Build Your
First Website

Prentice Hall
is an imprint of

Harlow, England • London • New York • Boston • San Francisco • Toronto • Sydney • Singapore • Hong Kong
Tokyo • Seoul • Taipei • New Delhi • Cape Town • Madrid • Mexico City • Amsterdam • Munich • Paris • Milan

PEARSON EDUCATION LIMITED

Edinburgh Gate
Harlow CM20 2JE
Tel: +44 (0)1279 623623
Fax: +44 (0)1279 431059
Website: www.pearsoned.co.uk

First published in Great Britain in 2011

ISBN: 978-0-273-74541-9

British Library Cataloguing-in-Publication Data
A catalogue record for this book is available from the British Library

Library of Congress Cataloging-in-Publication Data
Kraynak, Joe.
  Build your first website in simple steps / Joe Kraynak.
       p. cm.
  ISBN 978-0-273-74541-9 (pbk.)
  1. Web site development--Amateurs' manuals. 2. Web sites--Design--Amateurs' manuals. I. Title.
  TK5105.888.K699 2011
  006.7--dc22
                          2010052035

10 9 8 7 6 5 4 3 2
15 14 13 12

Designed by pentacorbig, High Wycombe
Typeset in 11/14 pt ITC Stone Sans by 30
Printed and bound in Great Britain by Scotprint, Haddington, East Lothian

Build Your First Website

Joe Kraynak

in Simple steps

Use your computer with confidence

Get to grips with practical computing tasks with minimal time, fuss and bother.

In Simple Steps guides guarantee immediate results. They tell you everything you need to know on a specific application; from the most essential tasks to master, to every activity you'll want to accomplish, through to solving the most common problems you'll encounter.

Helpful features

To build your confidence and help you to get the most out of your computer, practical hints, tips and shortcuts feature on every page:

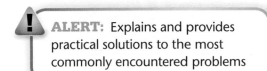 **ALERT:** Explains and provides practical solutions to the most commonly encountered problems

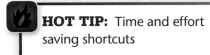 **HOT TIP:** Time and effort saving shortcuts

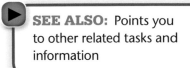 **SEE ALSO:** Points you to other related tasks and information

 **DID YOU KNOW?** Additional features to explore

WHAT DOES THIS MEAN?
Jargon and technical terms explained in plain English

Practical. Simple. Fast.

Author's acknowledgements:

Special thanks to Katy Robinson and Steve Temblett for choosing me to author this book and to Joli Ballew, Emma Devlin, Michelle Clark and the talented team at Prentice Hall and Pearson for transforming a good book into a great one. Thanks to Neil Salkind and Studio B for presenting me with this opportunity and handling all of the assorted details so that I could focus on my work. Thanks to the creative souls who have built the software and created the websites that have made all of this possible. Finally, thanks to Conor Temblett for finding the great cover image.

Publisher's acknowledgements:

We are grateful to the following for permission to reproduce copyright material:

Screenshots on pages 3, 4, 8, 9, 18, 54, 55, 56, 57, 58, 59, 60, 61, 62, 63, 64, 83, 84, 85, 86, 87, 89, 90, 91, 92, 94, 98, 99, 100, 101, 109, 110, 113, 114, 115, 116, 117, 118, 123, 124, 125, 126, 127, 128, 129, 130, 131, 132, 133, 134, 135, 139, 140, 141, 142, 143, 146, 147, 148, 149, 150, 151, 155, 156, 157, 158, 177, 178, 182, 183, 184, 185, 186, 187, 191, 193, 194, 195, 196, 197, 198, 199, 200, 201, 202, 203, 205, 212, 213, 214, 215, 220, 222, 223, 224, 225, 238, 243, 244, 245, 246, 248, 250, 253, 254, 255 and 257 from WordPress, Automattic, Inc; Screenshots on pages 21, 44, 45, 46, 47, 119 and 191 from FileZilla, licensed under the GNU General Public License, version 2, http://creativecommons.org/licenses/by-sa/3.0/deed.en; Screenshots on pages 26, 29, 30, 31, 32, 33, 34, 35, 36, 39, 40, 41, 42, 43, 48, 51, 52, 53, 93, 108, 243, 249 and 251 from Bluehost.com; Screenshot on page 67 from http://www.olawojtowicz.com/, website designed by OMdeSIGN.co.uk – Creative web design studio from London; Screenshot on page 67 from http://www.grantmacdonald.com, with permission from Grant Macdonald and website designed by OMdeSIGN.co.uk; Screenshot on page 68 from www.theadvisory.co.uk, website designed by OMdeSIGN.co.uk; Screenshot on page 68 from www.inspiritlondon.com, website designed by OMdeSIGN.co.uk; Screenshot on page 70 from www.malabar-restaurant.co.uk, website designed by OMdeSIGN.co.uk; Screenshot on page 70 from www.salthouses.com, website designed by OMdeSIGN.co.uk; Screenshot on page 71 from Yoga for the Mind, http://www.yogaforthemind.info, website designed by OMdeSIGN.co.uk; Screenshot on page 71 from http://www.enjoyingitaly.com, website designed by OMdeSIGN.co.uk; Screenshots on pages 78, 79 and 80 from ColorZilla Color Picker, with permission from Alex Sirota; Screenshots on page 102 from http://www.digitalwestex.com/gallery, website content Header Art and Wallpapers are reused under Creative Commons Attribution-ShareAlike 3.0 Unported, http://creativecommons.org/licenses/by-sa/3.0/deed.en; Screenshot on page 204 from YouTube, with permission from YouTube LLC.

Microsoft screen shots reprinted with permission from Microsoft Corporation.

In some instances we have been unable to trace the owners of copyright material, and we would appreciate any information that would enable us to do so.

in Simple steps

Contents at a glance

Contents

3 Transfer files with FTP

4 Set up a content management system

9 Accessorise your site with plugins

10 Add and format pages and posts with HTML

11 Configure a template with cascading style sheets (CSS)

14 Test and improve your site's speed

15 Raise your site's search engine profile

16 Manage your site with Google Webmaster Tools and Analytics

17 Generate income from your site

Top 10 Website Problems Solved

Top 10 Website Tips

Tip 1: Build a free Google site

Google sites enables you to create a free hosted website. While this may not be the best long-term strategy, it is a good way to learn the basics.

1 Go to www.google.com/sites and click Create new site.

2 Follow the onscreen cues to create your site.

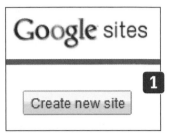

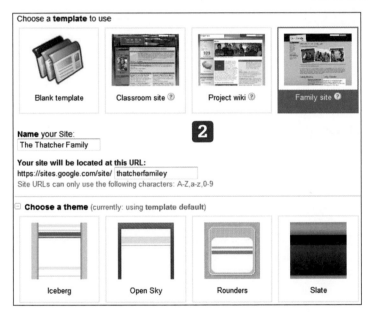

ALERT: You must be signed in to your free Google account to create a site. To create an account and sign in, visit www.google.co.uk.

WHAT DOES THIS MEAN?

Hosted website: a website that is built online, as opposed to creating the site on your computer and then uploading (copying) files to the Web.

Tip 2: Create a static website with WordPress

WordPress is a blogging platform, but you can use it to create a static website (without a blog).

1. Log in to WordPress and open the Pages menu.
2. Click Add New.
3. Type a page title for your site's opening page.
4. Click Publish.
5. Open the Settings menu and click Reading.
6. Click A static page.
7. Select the page to use as your front page.
8. Click Save Changes.

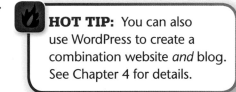
HOT TIP: You can also use WordPress to create a combination website *and* blog. See Chapter 4 for details.

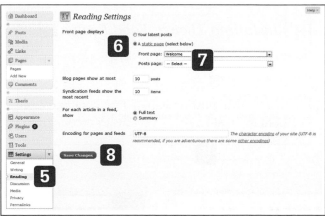

WHAT DOES THIS MEAN?

Blog: short for 'Web log', a site that contains regular posts arranged in reverse chronological order.

Tip 3: Change themes in WordPress

Plenty of free themes are available for WordPress and you can find many of them without having to leave it.

1 In WordPress, open the Appearance menu and click Themes.

2 Click Install Themes.

3 Click one of links near the top to browse the collection.

4 Click Install next to the desired theme.

5 Activate the theme.

WHAT DOES THIS MEAN?

Theme: a collection of files that control the appearance and layout of a site and may also add features.

HOT TIP: You can search or browse a collection of more than 1000 free themes at http://wordpress.org/extend/themes.

Tip 4: Choose an attractive colour scheme

Color Scheme Designer online at http://colorschemedesigner.com can help you choose harmonious colours for your site.

1 Go to http://colorschemedesigner.com.

2 Click a colour scheme type: mono, complement, triad, tetrad, analogic or accented analogic.

3 Drag the circles on the colour wheel to select the desired colours.

4 Rest the mouse pointer on Export and click HTML+CSS.

5 Color Scheme Designer displays the colour palette with hex codes for the colours.

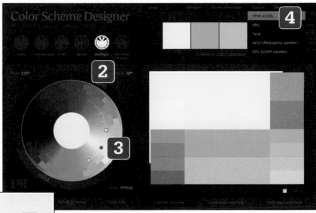

Primary Color:	FFFF00	BFBF30 BFBF30	A6A600 A6A600	FFFF40	FFFF73
Secondary Color A:	9FEE00 9FEE00	86B32D 86B32D	679B00 679B00	B9F73E B9F73E	C9F76F C9F76F
Secondary Color B:	FFD300 FFD300	BFA730 BFA730	A68900 A68900	FFDE40 FFDE40	FFE773 FFE773

 HOT TIP: To see the scheme on a sample Web page, click the 'Light page example' or 'Dark page example' option in the lower right corner of the screen.

 HOT TIP: Drag the darkest circle to move all of the circles and then drag the lighter circles to make finer adjustments.

Tip 5: Create a custom banner

You can use BannerFans at http://bannerfans.com to create an attractive header image to display at the top of your site.

1 Go to http://bannerfans.com and choose a background colour and gradient or upload an image.

2 Add and style text.

3 Add drop shadows and special text effects.

4 Add a border.

5 Download your banner.

HOT TIP: You can obtain free header art images from Digital Westex at www.digitalwestex.com/gallery and other online galleries.

DID YOU KNOW? WordPress enables you to upload the header image you want to use on your site from your computer.

Tip 6: Prepare photos for your site

Prior to uploading images, adjust their quality and size using photo editing software. This task shows how to prepare a photo in Picasa.

1 Open the photo in Picasa.

2 Click I'm Feeling Lucky.

3 Click Export.

4 Choose a folder to export to.

5 Specify image size and quality.

6 Click Export.

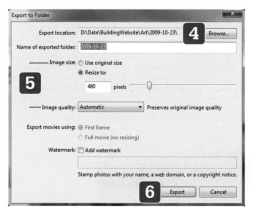

 HOT TIP: You can download Picasa for free from http://picasa.google.com.

 HOT TIP: To use only a portion of the image, crop as desired prior to exporting it.

Tip 7: Add a YouTube video

You can easily add a YouTube video to any Web page or blog post by copying the video's embed code and pasting it in your page or post source code.

1 On YouTube, copy the video's embed tag.

2 Create your page or post and change to HTML view.

3 Paste the embed code you copied in the previous task where you want the video to appear.

 HOT TIP: If you do not want to post your video on a sharing site, consider installing a plugin such as FLV Embed, which enables you to host videos on your own site. See Chapter 9 for more about plugins.

? DID YOU KNOW?

With the new HTML5 <video> element, soon you will be able to insert videos as easily as inserting images. As long as the video is in the proper format, browsers will be able to play it without a plugin or YouTube.

Tip 8: Configure your site with widgets

WordPress includes a collection of widgets that you can add to any sidebar simply by dragging and dropping them into the sidebar of your choice.

1 Open the Appearance menu and click Widgets.

2 Expand the destination sidebar box.

3 Drag the widget to the sidebar and drop it in place.

? DID YOU KNOW?

A theme may have two sidebars and allow you to use one or both of them.

▶ SEE ALSO: After dropping a widget in a sidebar box, the widget may expand and prompt you to enter settings. The next tip shows you how to enter settings.

⚠ ALERT: If you have difficulty working with widgets – such as a widget not appearing where you dropped it – try a different Web browser.

Tip 9: Examine source code with Firebug

To view the HTML tags and CSS styles that control the position and appearance of an element, use Firebug to inspect the element.

1 Open the Web page that contains the element you want to inspect.

2 Click the Firebug icon.

3 Click the Inspect Element button.

4 Click the element you want to inspect.

5 Check the element's HTML.

6 Identify the element's selector and style declarations.

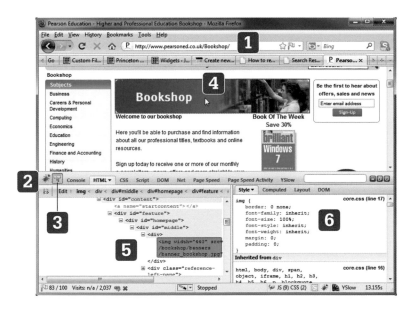

 HOT TIP: If that grey box gets in the way, you can drag it out of the way. You can also click the Layout tab just above the CSS style pane to view a graphic of the object's padding, border and margin.

 HOT TIP: Use Firebug to troubleshoot problems with HTML and CSS when an element is not appearing as you expect.

Tip 10: Test your website's performance

Several websites will test Web page loading times for you and indicate which elements on a page take the longest time to load. Find out below how to test page loading speed at http://pingdom.com.

1 Go to http://tools.pingdom.com.

2 Type or paste the address of a page on your site.

3 Click Test Now.

4 Note the results.

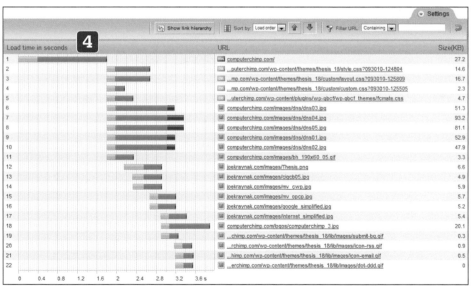

 HOT TIP: Test more than once over a period of time. Test results may be affected by factors other than those related to your site, such as traffic on the test site.

 DID YOU KNOW?
You can test page speed at other sites as well, including http://iwebtool.com/speed_test.

1 Know your options

Introduction

When the Web was in its infancy, there was only one way developers could create a website: they would type the source code for each page in a plain text file with the .html filename extension and then upload the files to a Web server using file transfer protocol (FTP). You can still build a website this way – see Code your site manually with HTML and CSS (at the end of this chapter), but now many other methods, tools and services are available to simplify the process. So, anyone with an Internet-enabled computer can build an attractive site in a matter of hours or even minutes. This chapter introduces you to the available options.

Build a free hosted website

A free hosted website service enables you to build and maintain a site online for free. These free services typically have restrictions on the number of pages, disk space and monthly traffic and your site address will begin with the service's domain name, such as google.com/site/.

1. Go to www.google.com/sites and click Create site.

2. Follow the onscreen cues to create your site.

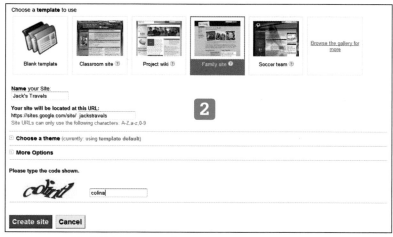

 ALERT: You must be signed in to your free Google account to create a site. To create an account and sign in, visit www.google.co.uk.

WHAT DOES THIS MEAN?

Web host: the service that provides a place on the Internet for websites.

Create a free hosted blog

Several services host blogs for free, including WordPress.com, Blogger.com and blog.co.uk. Here you will learn how to start blogging on Blogger.

1 Sign into your Google account at www.blogger.com and click CREATE YOUR BLOG NOW.

2 Follow the onscreen cues to create your blog and select a template.

SEE ALSO: Chapter 10 for details on how to post entries to a blog.

? DID YOU KNOW?
Google owns Blogger, so access both services through your Google account.

WHAT DOES THIS MEAN?

Blog: short for 'Web log', a blog is a site on which you post entries regularly and visitors are allowed to comment on your posts. Posts are typically arranged in reverse chronological order – the most recent first.

Use a Web hosting service

A standard Web hosting service (such as www.yoursite.co.uk) allows you to register your own domain name and use any number of tools to build and manage your website or blog.

1 Register a unique domain name.

2 Install a blogging platform or a content management system.

3 Enhance your site with additional components.

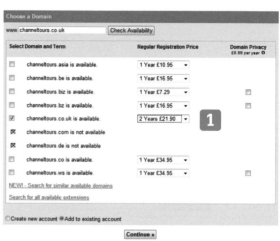

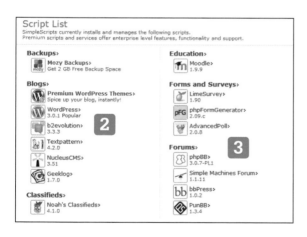

▶ **SEE ALSO:** Chapter 2, which shows how to get started with a Web hosting service.

WHAT DOES THIS MEAN?

Blogging platform: a type of content management system designed for posting regular entries and enabling visitors to comment on them.

Content management system (CMS): software that enables you to create and manage a site online, alone or in collaboration with others.

Build online with a content management system

An account with a Web hosting service typically includes free access to blogging platforms and other content management systems (CMS) that you can use to build and manage your site online.

1 Log in to your CMS.

2 Click the option to create a new page or post.

3 Type and format your page or post.

4 Publish your page or post.

SEE ALSO: Chapter 4 for instructions on how to install and use a CMS.

? DID YOU KNOW?
By choosing a different CMS theme, you completely change the appearance of your site.

? DID YOU KNOW?
One of the main benefits of a content management system is that several people can collaborate on site creation and management from locations anywhere around the world.

Build offline with a Web design application

A common way to build a site is to use a web design application on your computer and then upload the files you create to your web server. This task provides an overview of the process using a free web authoring program called KompoZer.

1 Run KompoZer and type the desired content.

2 Insert links, images, tables or forms.

3 Apply formatting.

4 Click Save to save the file.

5 Click Publish to upload your files to a Web server.

? DID YOU KNOW?
You can download KompoZer at http://kompozer.net.

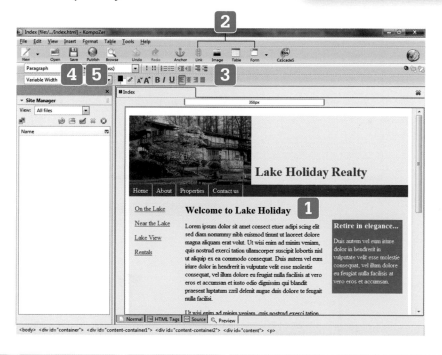

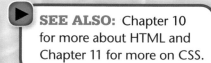

! ALERT: To use most Web design programs effectively, you really need to know how to use cascading style sheets (CSS) and hypertext markup language (HTML).

▶ SEE ALSO: Chapter 10 for more about HTML and Chapter 11 for more on CSS.

Code your site manually with HTML and CSS

The most difficult way to build a site is to type all of the HTML source code and CSS style rules using a plain text editor, such as Notepad or TextMate, as demonstrated in this task.

1 Open a text editor and type the HTML source code for your Web page.

2 Save the page as a text only file with the .htm or .html filename extension.

3 Type CSS style rules in a separate document.

4 Save the style sheet as a text only file with the .css filename extension.

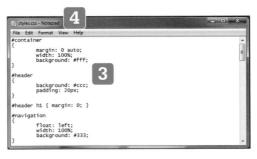

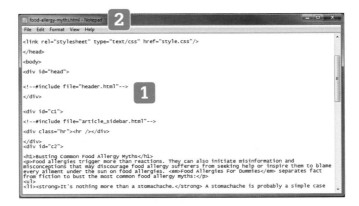

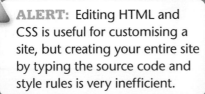

ALERT: Editing HTML and CSS is useful for customising a site, but creating your entire site by typing the source code and style rules is very inefficient.

HOT TIP: Even if you want to hand-craft your pages with HTML and CSS, use an HTML and CSS editor to avoid errors. With these applications, you can insert ready-made codes rather than have to type every character.

5 Link your HTML documents to your style sheet file.

 6 Upload your HTML documents and style sheet to your Web server.

? DID YOU KNOW?
Almost all Web design applications, HTML editors, CMSs and blogging platforms allow you to edit the HTML and CSS behind the Web pages if necessary.

▶ SEE ALSO: Chapter 10 for more on HTML and Chapter 11 for more on CSS.

2 Get started with a Web hosting service

Introduction

I strongly encourage you to build your site via a Web hosting service rather than trying to save money with a free hosted website or blog. You not only gain access to more powerful Web design and management tools but also build a permanent home on the Web with its own, unique address.

With a hosting service, you also obtain e-mail accounts with matching domain names. For example, if your site address is www.yoursite.co.uk, you may set up numerous e-mail accounts with addresses such as helen@yoursite.co.uk, steve@yoursite.co.uk and joli@yoursite.co.uk. This gives you a stronger presence on the Internet and enables you to promote your site through your e-mail address.

When you are getting started, you may not know what to expect from a Web hosting service. This chapter takes you on a tour and shows you how to perform several essential tasks.

Find a Web hosting service

Before you start building a website or blog, you need to find a service to host your site and provide the Web design and management tools required. Follow these steps to search for hosting services.

1 Search the Web for 'web host ranking'.

2 Click a link for one of the hosting service review or rating sites.

3 Write down the names of several services listed.

HOT TIP: Ask business associates and friends which hosting services they use and how they like them. You may also ask others on Facebook or Twitter or via e-mail.

ALERT: Top-ranked hosting services may not necessarily be the best for your needs. Perform additional research, as explained next.

Research a Web hosting service

Research each Web hosting service on your list to find the one you deem to be the best.

1 Visit your preferred Web hosting service's website to gather more information about the features it offers.

2 Visit the websites of the other candidates on your list and compare features.

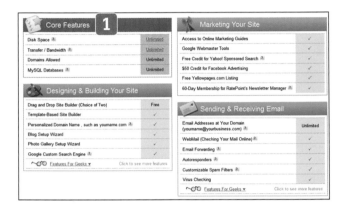

DID YOU KNOW?

Most good hosting services offer comparable features, so your choice will probably hinge on the company's reputation for quality and service.

ALERT: Make sure your chosen service offers WordPress (blog) installation and support. Most of the examples in this book focus on WordPress for site design and management.

Create an account

Before you can start using a hosting service, you must create an account and provide payment information – typically a credit card number. The following steps show you the process for iPage at www.ipage.com.

1 Visit the hosting service's home page.

2 Click the link to sign up or open an account.

3 If prompted to specify a domain name, type the name you want to use and click Continue.

4 Enter your contact information.

5 Enter your payment information.

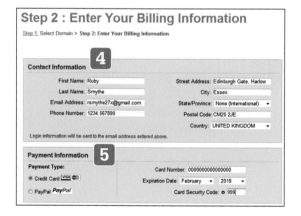

ALERT: All hosting services are different, so the steps required are likely to vary depending on the hosting service you choose.

HOT TIP: Before opening an account, search the Web for special deals or coupon codes for the hosting service – they may save you some money!

6 Select any additional features you desire or deselect features you do not want.

7 Click the button to check out and follow any additional instructions.

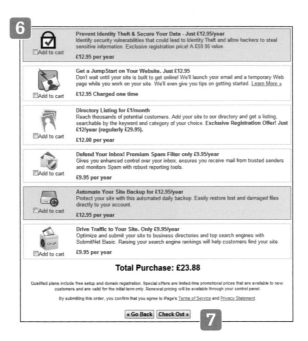

 HOT TIP: Your internet service provider (ISP) – the service you use to connect to the Internet – may include a free host website in your monthly subscription.

 ALERT: Most hosting services require either a one- or two-year commitment or offer a big monthly discount if you pay for one or two years of service in advance.

 HOT TIP: Many hosting services have loyalty or incentive schemes that enable you to earn money from referrals. Consider signing up for these and placing a link on your site that lets people know which service hosts your site.

Explore the hosting service's control panel

Web hosting services typically have a control panel (often cPanel) that provides a graphical interface for navigating the site and accessing features. Take a tour of your hosting service's control panel, to see what the service offers. The steps below are for using Bluehost's cPanel.

1 Sign in to your Web hosting account.

2 Use Preferences to change contact or billing information or your password.

3 Use the Mail options to create and manage your e-mail accounts.

4 Use the Files options to transfer files between your computer and the Web server.

5 Use the Domains options to register additional domain names and manage your domains.

6 Use the Software/Services options to install software and tools to build and manage your site.

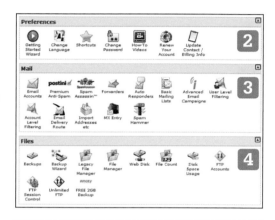

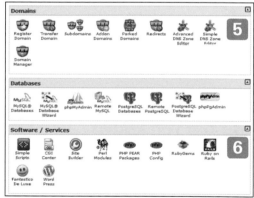

 ALERT: Not all hosting services use cPanel (iPage uses H-Sphere, for example), but the purpose is the same – to provide more intuitive access to features.

HOT TIP: Check the control panel and online help for tutorials or videos to help you get started with the more popular features.

 DID YOU KNOW?
You can safely ignore most of the options on the control panel. You may need only about ten of them and use only four to six regularly.

Register a domain name

You may have registered a domain name when you opened your Web hosting account. You can register additional domain names and manage them through your account.

1 Sign in to your Web hosting service's control panel.

2 Click Register Domain.

3 Type the domain name and suffix, if applicable.

4 Click Check and follow the onscreen instructions to complete the process.

 ALERT: If someone has already registered the domain name you want, you must choose a different name.

 HOT TIP: Keep it short. A good domain name is descriptive, but easy to remember and type.

 DID YOU KNOW?
You may build and manage multiple sites through a single Web hosting account by storing each site's files in a separate directory (folder) and assigning each folder a domain name.

 ALERT: Although your first domain name registration may be free, each one you add costs an additional annual registration fee.

WHAT DOES THIS MEAN?

Domain name: a descriptive, easy-to-remember Internet name or address.

Create a subdomain

By adding a prefix to your domain, you can create additional subdomains, each of which can be used to reference a separate site or component of a site. For example, if your domain name is yoursite.co.uk, you can create the subdomain store.yoursite.co.uk to add an online store.

1 Sign in to your Web hosting service's control panel.

2 Click Subdomains.

3 Type the prefix for your subdomain.

4 Select the primary subdomain, if not already shown.

5 Type a name for the folder in which to store the subdomain's files.

6 Click Create.

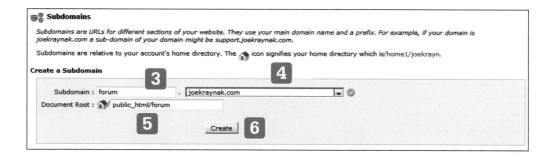

 ALERT: You do not need to create a separate subdomain for a blog. Chapter 4 shows how to create a blog and website combined on your primary domain using WordPress.

WHAT DOES THIS MEAN?

Subdomain: an offshoot of the main domain used to create distinct sections of a site.

HOT TIP: Consider using a subdomain for each section of your site, including store, chat, blog, forum, support and photos.

Assign an add-on domain

To manage more than one website, each with its own distinct domain name, from one hosting account, you must assign each domain as an add-on domain with a separate directory (folder). The steps below demonstrate the process using Bluehost.

1 Sign in to your Web hosting service's control panel.

2 Click Addon Domains.

3 Choose the domain you want to assign and verify ownership, if applicable.

4 Click the Addon Domain option.

5 Choose or type the name of a directory for the add-on domain.

6 Type a subdomain prefix for the new domain.

7 Click Add Domain.

> **! ALERT:** If you assigned a domain to a folder during the registration process, you do not need to do this.

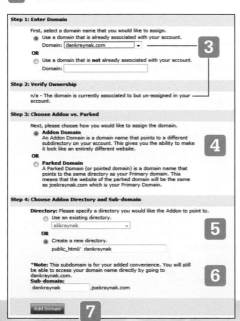

> **? DID YOU KNOW?**
>
> The folder in which you store the domain's files remains invisible. When visitors go to www.pleasant.meadows.co.uk, for example, they may be accessing files in a folder named stinkyfish, but they will not see the folder.

> **? DID YOU KNOW?**
>
> If a domain is registered with another service, you can use these steps to add it to your account. You will need to perform additional steps through the other service, however, to verify your ownership of the domain.

WHAT DOES THIS MEAN?

Add-on domain: a completely separate domain, with its files stored in a separate directory and having its own content, databases, e-mail accounts and so on.

Park a domain

You may want to register multiple domains and have them all access the same site. To do so, you park the secondary domains.

1 Sign in to your Web hosting service's control panel.

2 Click Parked Domains.

3 Choose the domain you want to park and verify ownership, if necessary.

4 Click the Parked Domain option and click Add Domain.

? DID YOU KNOW?

When you register a domain, your Web host may automatically park the domain on your account.

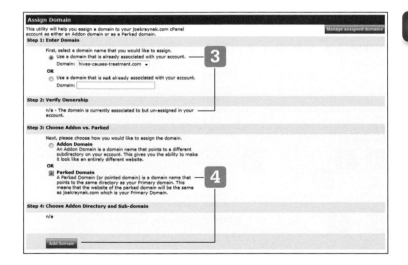

HOT TIP: If you are not going to develop a site on one of your domains and do not need it to point to your primary domain, consider parking it with a domain parking service, where it can generate income in the form of pay-per-click advertising. Search the Web for 'domain parking service'.

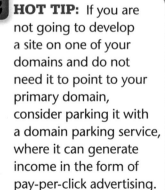

WHAT DOES THIS MEAN?

Parked domain: a domain that's automatically redirected to the primary domain on the same account. When someone tries to access the parked domain, the site located at the primary domain appears.

Create a redirect

If you move your site to a new domain or change the location of one or more files on your site, create a redirect to ensure traffic from the previous location is directed to the new location, then you will not lose traction with search engines that have already indexed your site.

1 Sign in to your Web hosting service's control panel.

2 Click Redirects.

3 Make sure Permanent (301) is selected.

4 Choose the domain you want to redirect.

5 To redirect a specific folder, type the path to the folder, including the folder's name.

6 Type the destination for the redirect, starting with 'http://'.

7 Click your www redirection preference, if available.

8 Click Wild Card Redirect to redirect all files in a directory to the same filenames in the redirects to folder.

9 Click Add.

? DID YOU KNOW?

You can redirect an entire domain, the contents of a folder or a single file to a different domain, folder or file.

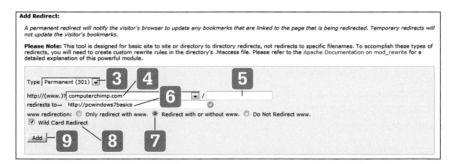

! ALERT: The method described here is for redirecting a domain or directory, not individual files. For steps to redirect individual files, consult your hosting service's help system.

? DID YOU KNOW?

A permanent (301) redirect updates the bookmarks in a visitor's browser and updates search engines. A temporary (302) redirect does not. Instead, it sends the browser to a different address, but browsers and search engines continue to try the original address in the future.

Check the server's status

Your Web hosting service's control panel may provide access to a utility for monitoring the status of the Web server that hosts your site. If your site is not accessible or seems slow, you may want to check the server's status.

1 Sign in to your Web hosting service's control panel.

2 Click Server Status.

3 Check for system alerts that may indicate a problem.

Server Status Notification
This system is designed to keep you informed of server outages. If you have multiple accounts, you may enter each one using this form, and status messages will appear for each account you've listed in the sections below. You may also remove them from this list using the link provided next to each server.
Note: All listed times are Mountain Time.

General systems alerts
(updated: 2010-09-23 08:10:38) no known issues: status ok

Alerts affecting all servers
(updated: 2010-09-23 08:10:38) no known issues: status ok

HOT TIP: Check the control panel for other utilities that enable you to monitor your service. A CPU throttling utility, if available, can help you check the frequency and duration of any throttling (see Did you know?) of your site.

DID YOU KNOW?
Most Web hosting services are shared, meaning your site shares a server with other customers' sites. Traffic on these other sites may affect your site's performance and vice versa. Some services throttle (slow down) sites when they consume more than their share of bandwidth.

WHAT DOES THIS MEAN?
Bandwidth: the amount of data an Internet connection can carry at any given time.

Create an e-mail account

Your Web hosting account very likely includes e-mail support, meaning you can create and manage e-mail accounts with addresses that include your domain name. The following steps show you how to create a new e-mail account.

1 Sign in to your Web hosting service's control panel.

2 Click Email Accounts.

3 Type the first part of the e-mail address you want to use for this account.

4 Choose the domain you want to use, if necessary.

5 Type a password in the Password and Password confirmation boxes.

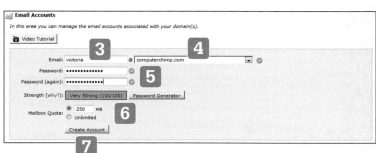

6 Set a mailbox quota, if desired.

7 Click Create Account.

 HOT TIP: Check out other e-mail features that your Web host provides, including spam filtering, e-mail forwarding and auto responders.

? DID YOU KNOW?

Creating an e-mail account may seem out of place in a book about building a website, but having an e-mail address with a domain that matches your site address helps to promote your site.

! ALERT: Setting an e-mail quota is a good means of protecting yourself from becoming overloaded with e-mail messages that contain large attachments.

 HOT TIP: Check your Web hosting service's help system for details on accessing your e-mail accounts via the Web or by using an e-mail client, such as Microsoft Outlook.

3 Transfer files with FTP

Introduction

Transferring files from your computer to the hosting service's file server is not one of the most exciting activities in building a website, but it is an essential task. Assuming that you build your site using a content management system (CMS), you may not need to do many file transfers, but you will need to upload photos and other images and you may need to upload and download individual files when customising or troubleshooting your site.

To transfer files, you use a file transfer protocol (FTP) client, which connects your computer to the file server and makes file transfer as easy as moving a file from one folder to another on your computer (FTP is a set of rules that govern the transfer of files on the Internet). Your Web hosting service is likely to provide its own FTP client or you can use a third-party application, such as FileZilla. This chapter demonstrates both methods.

Before you perform any steps in this chapter, though, make sure you're logged in to your Web hosting account.

Access your hosting service's FTP features

Your Web hosting service is very likely to feature its own FTP client that you can access from the control panel. Here you will see how to do this and be introduced to the FTP interface.

1 On your hosting provider's control panel, click Unlimited FTP.

2 Navigate disk drives and folders on your computer.

3 Navigate folders on the server.

4 Transfer selected files and folders in the desired direction, indicated by the arrows – that is, from your computer to the server or from the server to your computer.

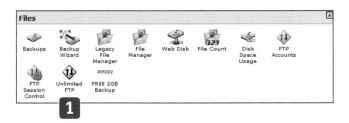

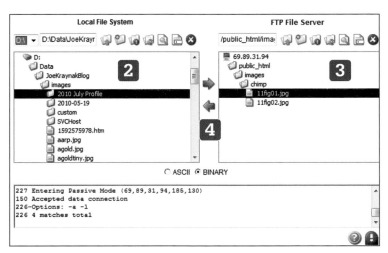

SEE ALSO: The remaining sections in this chapter show how to navigate and transfer files and folders between your computer and the server.

WHAT DOES THIS MEAN?

File server: a high-capacity storage device on a network that provides access to shared files and folders. In this case, the network is the Internet.

File transfer protocol (FTP): a set of rules that govern the transfer of files on the Internet.

Navigate folders on your server

To transfer files and folders, you must first access them. Here's how.

1 Double-click a folder to open it.

2 Click the Up One Folder icon to move up one level in the directory tree.

3 Click the Create New Folder icon to create a new folder inside the currently open folder.

4 Click the Rename icon at the end to rename the selected file or folder.

5 Click the delete symbol to delete the selected file or folder.

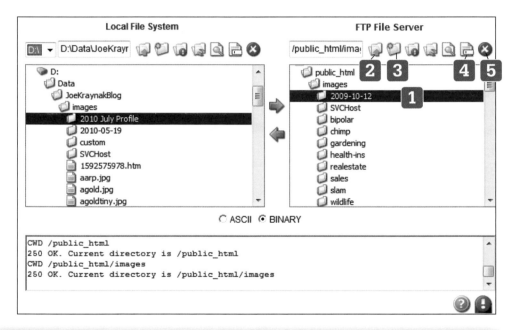

> **? DID YOU KNOW?**
> The pane below the two folder lists displays the status of each action you perform.

> **! ALERT:** Avoid accessing any folders or files if you are uncertain what they are for. Deleting, renaming or moving a system file or folder may harm your account's functionality.

> **? DID YOU KNOW?**
> Your website files and folders will be stored in a folder named something like public_html to make them publicly accessible.

Create a new folder

You may need to create a new folder on the file server into which you will place the files and folders that comprise your site or a folder in which to store images. Follow the steps below to learn how to do this.

1 Double-click the folder in which you want the new folder to be created.

2 Click the Create New Folder icon.

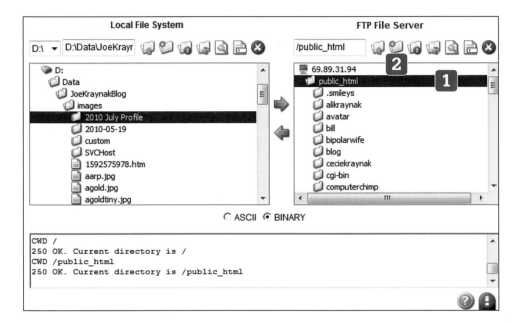

3 Click the Rename icon and type a name for the folder.

4 Click OK.

ALERT: Create folders for your website in the public_html folder so that they will be publicly accessible.

ALERT: When naming a folder, type the name in all lower-case characters, with no spaces, using only letters and numbers. You can use a dash or underline instead of a space.

Upload files with FTP

You can upload files to the file server to place them on the Internet. Placing files in the public_html folder or one of its subfolders makes them accessible on the Web.

1 Navigate to the folder on your computer where the folder or files you want to upload are stored.

2 Navigate to the folder on the file server that you want to upload the folder(s) or file(s) to.

3 Select the file(s) or folder(s) on your computer that you want to upload.

4 Click the Upload button (top arrow).

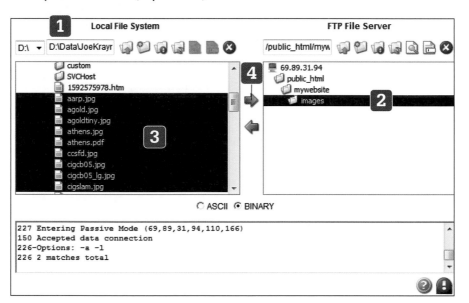

5 Wait until the upload has been completed.

WHAT DOES THIS MEAN?

Upload: to copy files from your computer to the file server.

? DID YOU KNOW?

The time required for the upload to complete varies depending on the amount of data and your connection speed.

Download files with FTP

You can download files from the file server to your computer to edit them or download files or folders to back them up.

1 Navigate to the disk and folder on your computer in which you want the downloaded folder(s) or file(s) to be stored.

2 Navigate to the folder on the file server where the folder or files you want to download are stored.

3 Select the file(s) or folder(s) on the file server that you want to download.

4 Click the Download button (bottom arrrow).

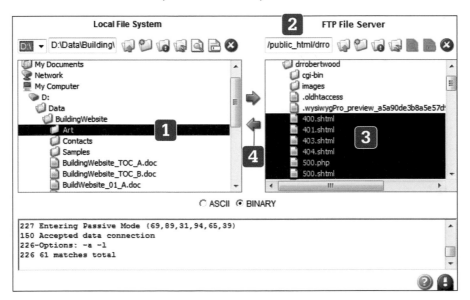

5 Wait until the download has been completed.

WHAT DOES THIS MEAN?

Download: to copy files from the file server to your computer.

HOT TIP: Before editing a file on the file server, download it, so that you have a copy of the original.

Install a dedicated FTP client

Instead of logging on to the control panel every time you want to transfer files, you can use an FTP client on your computer to transfer files. Here's how to download and install FileZilla.

1 Use your Web browser to go to http://filezilla-project.org.

2 Click Download FileZilla Client.

3 Click the link for the version you want.

4 Click Save File and save the file to your computer.

5 Double-click the downloaded file and follow the onscreen instructions to install FileZilla.

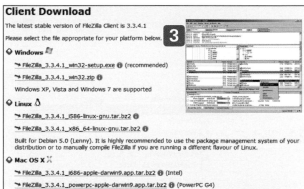

DID YOU KNOW?

FileZilla is the most popular free FTP client, but not the only one. Others include WinSCP for Windows (http://winscp.net), FireFTP (an add-on for Mozilla Firefox, http://fireftp.mozdev.org) and Cyberduck for Mac OS X (http://cyberduck.ch).

Enter login information

Your FTP client needs login information to connect to your file server. In FileZilla, the best approach is to use Site Manager to create an entry for the file server and here's how you do it.

 Run FileZilla, open the File menu and click Site Manager.

2 Click New Site.

3 Type a name for the site.

4 Type the address of your file server and a port number if required.

5 Open the Logon Type list and click Normal.

6 Type your username and password.

7 Click Connect or OK.

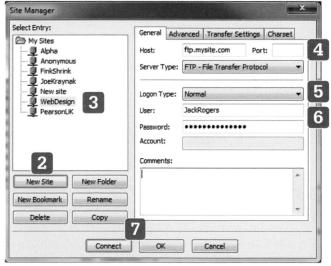

! ALERT: Check your hosting service's help system to find out the FTP server's address and port number, if required.

45

? DID YOU KNOW?

Your username is typically shown next to the control panel after you log in. Also, your password is probably the same password you use to log in to the control panel.

🔥 HOT TIP: In Site Manager, click the Advanced tab to specify a default folder (directory) for your computer and the file server (remote directory), so that FileZilla automatically opens the folders you most frequently access whenever you log in.

Connect to your FTP server

After you enter login information for your FTP server, connecting to your server is very easy. You simply select the entry you created from a list.

1 Run FileZilla and click the down arrow to the right of the Open the Site Manager icon.

2 Click the entry for your FTP server.

HOT TIP: Click the Open the Site Manager icon rather than the arrow next to it to display the Site Manager with more connection options.

HOT TIP: To connect to the same server that you connected to last time you used FileZilla, click the 'R' button.

DID YOU KNOW? To disconnect from the server, click the Disconnect button – the button with the red 'X' on it.

Upload and download files

The process of uploading and downloading files with a dedicated FTP client is very similar to the process used when accessing your hosting service's FTP utility.

1 Navigate to the desired folder on your computer.

2 Navigate to the desired folder on the FTP server.

3 Select the file(s) or folder(s) you want to upload or download.

4 Right-click one of the selected items and click Upload or Download.

5 Wait until the upload or download has been completed.

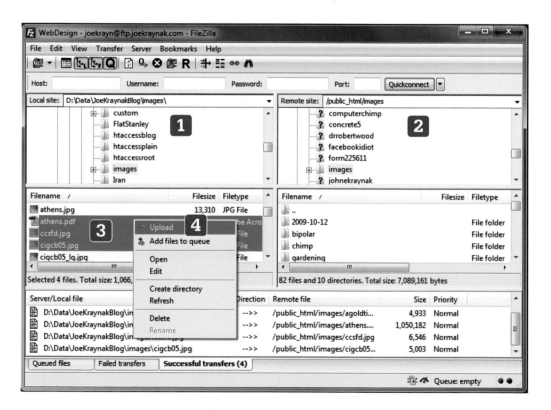

! ALERT: As you upload or download files, the folder or file lists may not update automatically. If you don't see a file or folder, click the Refresh button.

? DID YOU KNOW?

Your FTP client will warn you if you are about to replace a file or folder with another that has the same name.

Create a new FTP account

To give someone else password-protected access to files on your FTP server, you must create a new FTP account with a login name and password, as follows.

1 On your hosting service's control panel, click FTP Accounts.

2 Type a single-word login name.

3 Type a password in both boxes.

4 Type the path to the folder you want to share, including its name.

5 Click Create FTP Account.

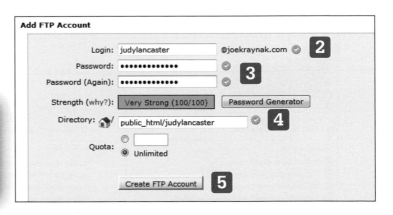

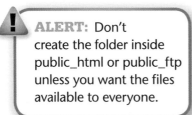

ALERT: Don't create the folder inside public_html or public_ftp unless you want the files available to everyone.

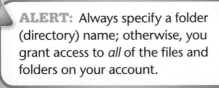

ALERT: Always specify a folder (directory) name; otherwise, you grant access to *all* of the files and folders on your account.

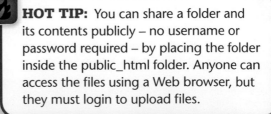

HOT TIP: You can share a folder and its contents publicly – no username or password required – by placing the folder inside the public_html folder. Anyone can access the files using a Web browser, but they must login to upload files.

4 Set up a content management system

Introduction

As explained in Chapter 1, a content management system (CMS) enables you to easily design and redesign your site, plus post and update its content. Before you can take advantage of a CMS, however, you must install one and enter a few basic settings.

The good news is that most Web hosting services provide a tool that you can use to install a CMS. Some hosting services specialise in one CMS, others let you choose. I recommend WordPress because it is simple to use and has many free themes, plugins and widgets for personalising and accessorising sites. In addition, you can use WordPress to build a website, blog or a combination of the two.

This chapter and others in this book demonstrate how to use WordPress to design, build and manage a site. Although the overall approach is similar in other CMSs, the steps vary significantly from it.

Explore your options

Your hosting service may provide access to numerous open source CMSs, including WordPress, Joomla, Drupal and Concrete5. Check the control panel, as shown below, to see which CMSs are available.

1 On your hosting provider's control panel, click the SimpleScripts or Fantastico button.

2 Check out the blog, content management and website builder options.

HOT TIP: To find out more about a CMS, click its icon for a brief introduction. This will typically include a link to the CMS's home page, where you can do further research.

DID YOU KNOW?

SimpleScripts and Fantastico are two commonly used utilities for installing website development software, but your hosting service may offer different utilities.

WHAT DOES THIS MEAN?

Open source: software that can be used and distributed free of charge.

Install WordPress

Assuming your Web hosting service provides an installation utility for WordPress, installing it is a snap, as the steps below demonstrate. Many hosting providers have an installation icon right on the main control panel.

1 On your hosting provider's control panel, click the WordPress icon.

2 Click Install.

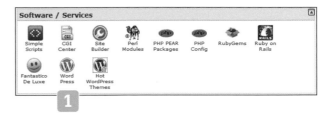

? **DID YOU KNOW?**

Installing WordPress in the past was a complicated process that required you to set up a database for it. The installation utilities we have today make the process much easier.

! **ALERT:** You may need to go through SimpleScripts or Fantastico to install WordPress, as explained in the previous section.

 HOT TIP: Install WordPress in a subdirectory with a cryptic name so unauthorised users will have difficulty guessing where to go to log in.

3 Type the name of the folder in which you want to store your site's files.

4 Click 'Click here to display' to display advanced options.

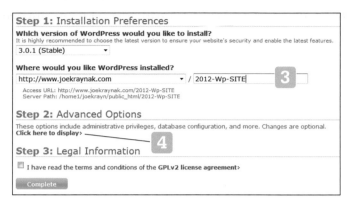

Step 1: Installation Preferences

Which version of WordPress would you like to install?
It is highly recommended to choose the latest version to ensure your website's security and enable the latest features.

3.0.1 (Stable)

Where would you like WordPress installed?

http://www.joekraynak.com   / 2012-Wp-SITE   3

Access URL: http://www.joekraynak.com/2012-Wp-SITE
Server Path: /home1/joekrayn/public_html/2012-Wp-SITE

Step 2: Advanced Options

These options include administrative privileges, database configuration, and more. Changes are optional.
Click here to display> — 4

Step 3: Legal Information

☐ I have read the terms and conditions of the GPLv2 license agreement>

Complete

5 Type a name for your site.

6 Type a username and password for logging in to WordPress.

7 Make sure Automatically create a new database is selected.

8 Read the licence agreement and click to indicate your agreement.

9 Click Complete.

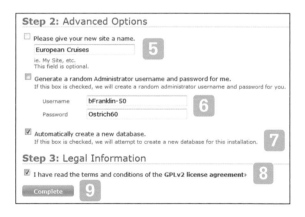

Step 2: Advanced Options

☐ Please give your new site a name.

European Cruises   5

ie. My Site, etc.
This field is optional.

☐ Generate a random Administrator username and password for me.
If this box is checked, we will create a random administrator username and password for you.

Username   bFranklin-50   6
Password   Ostrich60

☑ Automatically create a new database.
If this box is checked, we will attempt to create a new database for this installation.   7

Step 3: Legal Information

☑ I have read the terms and conditions of the GPLv2 license agreement>   8

Complete   9

! ALERT: Write down the folder in which you installed WordPress, as well as your username and password, then store the information in a safe, secure location.

? DID YOU KNOW? As soon as you install WordPress, you have a site on the Web and can visit it by going to the folder in which you installed WordPress.

Log in to WordPress

Before you can do anything in WordPress, you must log in, as shown below. Logging in displays the WordPress Dashboard, which provides access to all the tools you need to design and build your site, then post its content.

1 In your Web browser, type the address to the WordPress installation folder, followed by '/wp-admin'.

2 Type your username.

3 Type your password.

4 Click Log In.

5 To log out, click Log Out.

> **SEE ALSO:** Enter your front page preference later in this chapter to learn how to transform a WordPress blog into a website or combination website and blog.

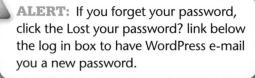

ALERT: If you forget your password, click the Lost your password? link below the log in box to have WordPress e-mail you a new password.

? DID YOU KNOW?
You can pull up the login screen by typing the address of your WordPress installation followed by either '/wp-admin' or '/wp-login.php'.

Navigate WordPress

After you log in to WordPress, you meet the WordPress Dashboard. The steps below show you how to navigate the Dashboard so you can access the numerous WordPress features.

1 Click the arrow to the right of a menu to display or hide its options.

2 Click the line between menus to expand or contract the menu titles.

3 Click an option to display its settings.

4 Click Screen Options to choose what WordPress displays on the current screen and how it displays the content.

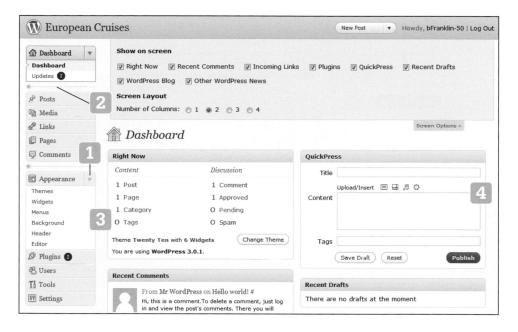

HOT TIP: You can click your site title (in the upper left-hand corner of the Dashboard) to visit your site.

HOT TIP: Click Help, near the upper right-hand corner of the Dashboard (but you can't see it here as it's only visible when the Screen Options panel has been minimised), to obtain assistance.

? DID YOU KNOW?

If you install plugins to add functionality to WordPress, they may add options to the Dashboard, as explained in Chapter 9.

Enter a privacy preference

Until you have a chance to design your site and add some content to it, you may want to make it invisible to search engines. To do this, change your site's privacy setting.

1 Log in to WordPress and open the Settings menu.

2 Click Privacy.

3 Click the I would like to block search engines, but allow normal visitors option.

4 Click Save Changes.

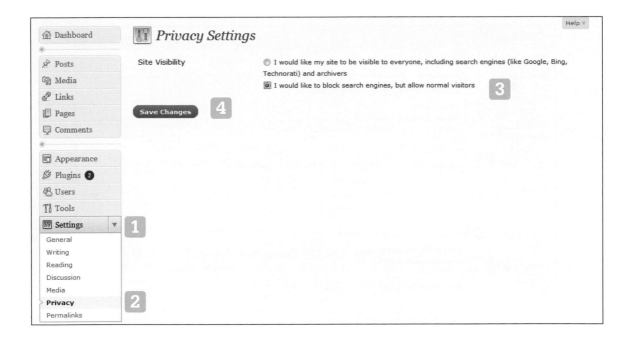

ALERT: Don't forget to change back to the original setting when your site is ready.

HOT TIP: If you would like to make your site inaccessible during development, consider installing the Maintenance Mode plugin. See Chapter 9 for details on plugins.

Enter a site title and tagline

Your site title and tagline tell users and search engines what your site is all about. You probably gave your site a title when installing WordPress, but you can change it at any time, as demonstrated in this task.

1️⃣ Log in to WordPress and open the Settings menu.

2️⃣ Click General.

3️⃣ Edit the site's title, if desired.

4️⃣ Type a brief but descriptive tagline.

5️⃣ Click Save Changes.

❓ DID YOU KNOW?
Depending on how you design your site, the title and tagline may or may not appear at the top of each web page on your site.

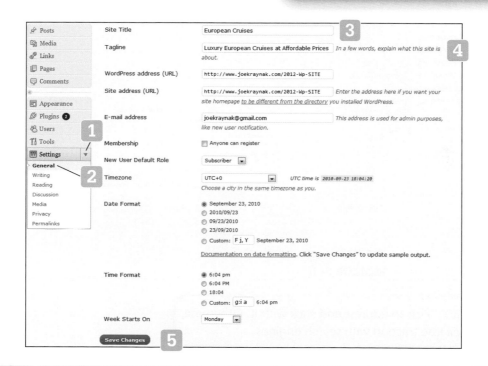

⚠️ ALERT: Your site title can be catchy and cryptic, but the tagline should contain key words that help search engines identify the content on your site and index it properly.

▶️ SEE ALSO: Chapter 7 for details on replacing the display of the site title and tagline with a header image and Chapter 11 for details on formatting the text in your site's title and tagline.

Enter the site's address

I recommend that you install WordPress in a separate folder (directory), then specify a different address for visitors to use to access your site. The following steps show you how to do this.

1 Log in to WordPress and open the Settings menu.

2 Click General.

3 Type the site's address for visitors to enter to access your site, starting with 'http://'.

4 Click Save Changes.

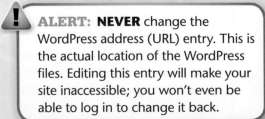
ALERT: Pick an address and stick with it. Otherwise, you will lose traction with search engines.

ALERT: NEVER change the WordPress address (URL) entry. This is the actual location of the WordPress files. Editing this entry will make your site inaccessible; you won't even be able to log in to change it back.

SEE ALSO: The domain specified in the site's address must be assigned to the folder in which WordPress is installed. See Chapter 2, Assign an add-on domain, for details. If you have already assigned the domain to a different folder, use the Domain Manager to unassign it first.

Enter your front page preference

Unless you specify otherwise, your blog is your front page – the first page visitors see when they access your site. You can choose to have a different page greet visitors.

1 Log in to WordPress and open the Pages menu.

2 Click Add New.

3 Type a page title for your site's opening page.

4 Click Publish.

5 Repeat steps 2 to 4 to create a separate page for your blog.

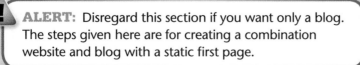

ALERT: If you do not want a blog on your site, do not create a page for the blog.

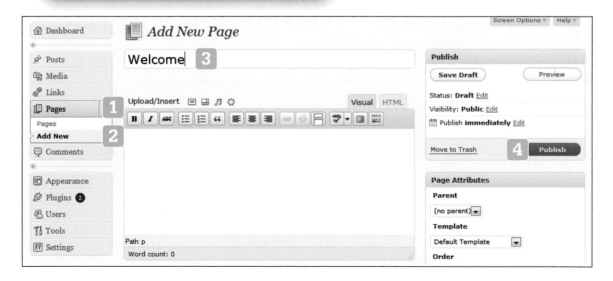

ALERT: Disregard this section if you want only a blog. The steps given here are for creating a combination website and blog with a static first page.

6 Open the Settings menu and click Reading.

7 Click the A static page option.

8 Select the page to use as your front page.

9 Select the page to use for your blog.

10 Click Save Changes.

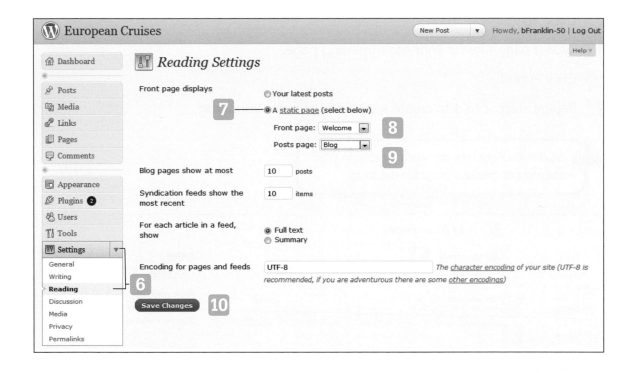

 DID YOU KNOW?

One of the best features of WordPress is that it enables you to create a static website, a blog or a combination of a website and a blog.

 SEE ALSO: Chapter 10 for detailed instructions on creating pages and posts.

Enter a permalinks preference

WordPress identifies pages and posts by number rather than filename, so, when you access a page, its address may appear as 'http://www.yoursite.co.uk/?p=15'. You can enter a permalinks setting to have your pages and posts identified by name. Here's how.

1 Log in to WordPress and open the Settings menu.

2 Click Permalinks.

3 Click one of the common settings or type a custom structure.

4 Click Save Changes.

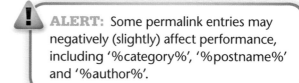

ALERT: Some permalink entries may negatively (slightly) affect performance, including '%category%', '%postname%' and '%author%'.

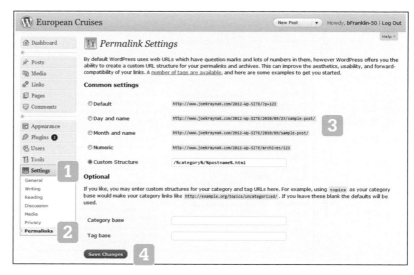

? DID YOU KNOW?

The custom structure used here – '/%category%/%postname%.html' – displays the post's category and name, followed by '.html'. You can include other items by using the following entries:

* **%year%** year of the post – 2012, for example

* **%monthnum%** month of the year – 07, for example

* **%day%** day of the month – 16, for example

* **%hour%** hour of the day – 18, for example

* **%minute%** minute of the hour – 35, for example

* **%second%** second of the minute – 27, for example

* **%post_id%** the post number without '?p='

* **%author%** author's name.

Adjust discussion settings

If you are building a blog, adjust the discussion settings, if desired, to control the management and display of comments that visitors may leave in response to your blog posts.

1 Log in to WordPress and open the Settings menu.

2 Click Discussion.

3 Enter your preferences.

4 Click Save Changes.

> **ALERT:** Placing too many restrictions on comments may discourage people from posting comments.

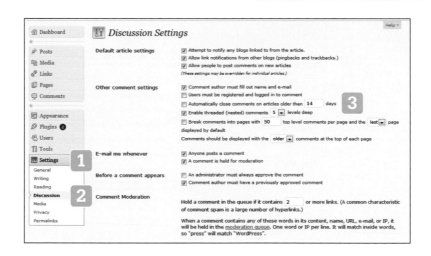

? DID YOU KNOW?
WordPress is set up to e-mail you whenever someone posts a comment. To change the e-mail address notifications are sent to, open the Settings menu and click General.

 SEE ALSO: You can use plugins to reduce comment spam without having to make your discussion settings overly restrictive. See Chapter 9 for details on plugins.

Edit your profile

You can edit information in your profile, including the name that appears next to your blog posts. Just follow the steps below.

1. Log in to WordPress, open the Users menu and click Your Profile.

2. Type your First Name in the box.

3. Type your Last Name in the next box.

4. Type a Nickname, if desired, in the third box.

5. Choose how you want your name displayed next to posts.

6. Edit other information and settings, as desired.

7. Click Update Profile.

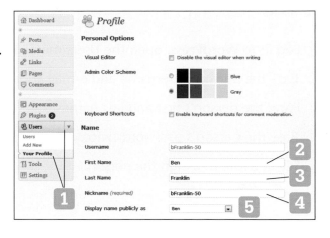

> **ALERT:** You cannot edit your user name. If you want to change it, create a new user as an administrator, then log in as the new user and delete the previous user.

> **? DID YOU KNOW?** You can also change your contact e-mail address and password via your profile settings.

> **HOT TIP:** You can use a photo of yourself or some other image as an avatar that appears next to your posts. For details on how to include an avatar, open the Users menu, click Avatars and scroll down to the bottom of the page.

Add a user

Suppose you want to manage a site with others to share the burden of posting and editing its content. You can do so by adding other users to WordPress. This is how you do it.

1 Log in to WordPress, open the Users menu and click Add New.

2 Type the person's username and e-mail address.

3 Enter the person's first and last names.

4 Type the person's password twice.

5 Select a role to assign the person.

6 Click Add User.

ALERT: Don't grant administrator access to just anyone – they can delete users, including you!

? DID YOU KNOW?

A user's role determines his or her WordPress access level:

- **subscribers** can read and post comments
- **contributors** can write and manage their own posts, but not publish posts or upload media
- **authors** can publish and manage their own posts
- **editors** can publish and manage their own and other users' posts
- **administrators** have full access.

5 Design an attractive colour scheme

Introduction

Some of the biggest decisions you make when designing a website relate to the colour scheme. In addition to making everything on the site appear attractive and readable, a colour scheme gives your site personality and evokes the desired emotional response from visitors.

Selecting the wrong colours can make text difficult to read, drive visitors from your site and perhaps send the wrong message, on an emotional level, about what your site is all about. The right colours make visitors feel at home, improve the appearance of your site and make its content easy to access.

In this chapter, you will learn about colours in theory and in practice, so you can choose a suitable colour scheme to implement on your site.

Use colours to set the tone and evoke emotion

On a subconscious level, colours evoke emotion. In Western cultures, for example, most people associate red with love, passion and excitement, while blue tends to soothe the emotions and convey trust. As you design your site, be aware of these colour associations and choose colours that set the desired tone.

1 Use a black-and-white colour scheme to convey mystery, purity, elegance, simplicity or death.

2 Use red to convey passion, danger, power or desire.

3 Use yellow, like sunshine, to convey a sense of happiness and joy.

 HOT TIP: Red, orange and yellow serve as excellent accent colours on dark backgrounds to call attention to specific items.

4 Use blue to convey intelligence, trust and tranquillity.

5 Use green to suggest freshness, growth, nature and plenitude.

? **DID YOU KNOW?**

Emotional reactions to colour are often rooted in culture. White may convey a sense of purity and peace in Western cultures, but some Eastern cultures associate it with death.

Use a colour wheel

Some colours look better together than others. To ensure that the colours you choose look attractive when combined in a colour scheme, consult the colour wheel.

1 For high contrast, consider complementary colours – that is, colours directly across from one another on the colour wheel.

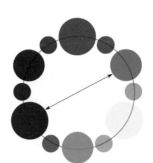

2 For more variation, use a split complementary colour scheme – one dominant colour and two colours adjacent to the dominant colour's complementary colour.

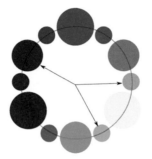

3 For a richer, more balanced design, use a triadic colour scheme – three colours equidistant from each other on the colour wheel.

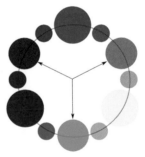

4 For the richest design, use a tetradic colour scheme – complementary colours plus a pair of complementary colours adjacent to them.

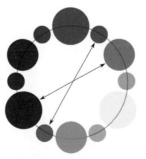

 ALERT: Avoid choosing colours that are *almost* opposite on the colour wheel. These colours are called discordant, because they tend to clash.

 HOT TIP: Analogous colours make a very attractive colour scheme, as well. Analogous colours are those that are next to each other on the colour wheel.

Explore sample colour schemes

Before creating a colour scheme for your site, visit others with colour schemes that convey the emotional tone you want for your website.

 Achromatic designs are very clean and simple.

 Add one colour to create an attractive monochromatic design.

HOT TIP: You can add colour to an achromatic site by using colour photos.

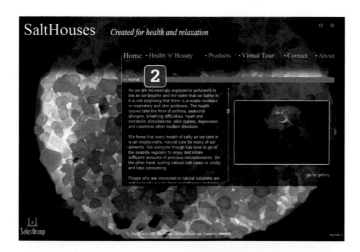

WHAT DOES THIS MEAN?

Achromatic: without colour, using only black, white and shades of grey.

HOT TIP: If you are creating a business site, visit your competitors' websites and think how you can make yours stand out from the others.

3 Analogous designs use colours next to one another on the colour wheel.

4 Complementary designs use complementary colours.

WHAT DOES THIS MEAN?

Neutral colour: muted colours that work well with all other colours. Neutral colours include shades of grey, brown and beige, along with white and black.

Use Color Scheme Designer

Some graphics programs include tools for generating attractive colour schemes. If you have no access to such tools, you can use Color Scheme Designer online (at http://colorschemedesigner.com).

1 Go to http://colorschemedesigner.com.

2 Click a colour scheme type: mono, complement, triad, tetrad, analogic or accented analogic.

3 Drag the circles on the colour wheel to select the desired colours.

4 Rest the mouse pointer on Export and click HTML+CSS.

5 Color Scheme Designer displays the colour palette you have chosen with hex codes for the colours.

HOT TIP: Drag the darkest circle to move all of the circles and then drag the lighter circles to make finer adjustments.

HOT TIP: To see the scheme on a sample Web page, click the 'Light page example' or 'Dark page example' option in the lower right-hand corner of the options screen.

Install ColorZilla for Firefox

ColorZilla is a plugin for the Mozilla Firefox web browser that enables you to identify the hex code for any colour on a website or image. This is valuable for creating your own colour schemes from existing websites and images.

1. Run Mozilla Firefox.
2. Click Tools, Add-ons.
3. Click Get Add-ons.
4. Search for ColorZilla.
5. Click Add to Firefox.

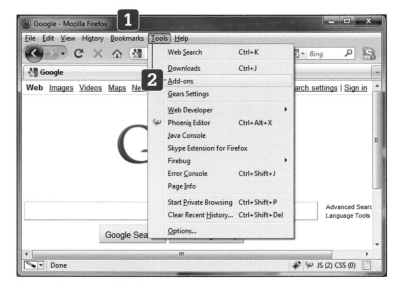

HOT TIP: To explore additional Firefox add-ons, visit http://addons.mozilla.org.

WHAT DOES THIS MEAN?

Add-on: a feature that enhances an application.

 DID YOU KNOW?

More than 5000 add-ons are available for Firefox.

6 Click ColorZilla.

7 Click Install Now.

8 When prompted, restart Firefox.

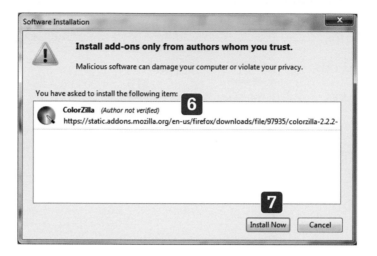

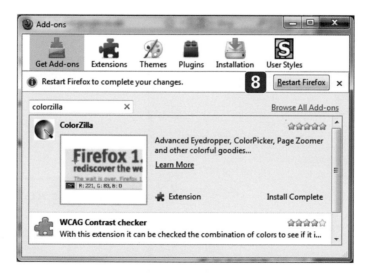

 ALERT: This task assumes Mozilla Firefox is installed. If you do not have the Firefox web browser, download and install it from www.mozilla.com.

Pick up colours from an image

If you have a logo, photograph or other colourful image that you want to use as the central image on your site, perhaps in the header area, you can base your colour scheme on it. Simply pick out colours from the image to use for lettering, backgrounds and so on.

1 In Firefox, click File, Open File.

2 Open the image file that contains the desired colours.

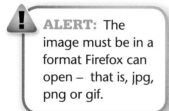

ALERT: The image must be in a format Firefox can open – that is, jpg, png or gif.

 HOT TIP: Nature photos are excellent for building colour schemes on, because the colours look good together.

3 Click the ColorZilla eyedropper icon.

4 Click the desired colour.

5 Open the ColorZilla menu and copy the hex code for your chosen colour.

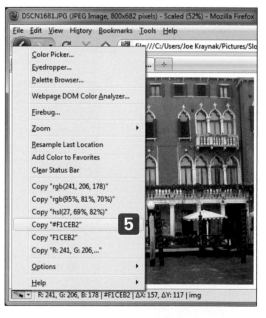

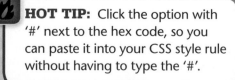

HOT TIP: Click the option with '#' next to the hex code, so you can paste it into your CSS style rule without having to type the '#'.

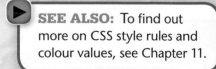

SEE ALSO: To find out more on CSS style rules and colour values, see Chapter 11.

Pick up colours from a Web page

If a website has a colour you want to match, use ColorZilla to pick up the colour's hex code from the page. You can then paste the hex code into your CSS style rule.

1 In Firefox, open the Web page that has the desired colour scheme.

2 Click the ColorZilla eyedropper icon.

3 Click the desired colour.

4 Open the ColorZilla menu and copy the hex code for the chosen colour.

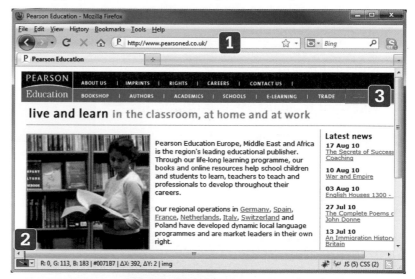

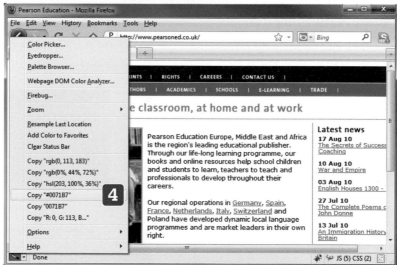

 ALERT: Do not use a colour scheme just because you like its appearance. Your scheme should promote your site's purpose.

HOT TIP: ColorZilla has more features than are covered here. To find out more, open ColorZilla's menu, point to Help and click Online help.

Change a colour's saturation

If a colour seems too intense, you can decrease the colour saturation without changing the actual colour so that then it will not overpower everything else on the page. This is especially useful when working with backgrounds because you want elements in the foreground to stand out.

1 Run Firefox and choose the colour you want to adjust.

2 Open the ColorZilla menu and click Palette Browser.

3 Increase or decrease the colour's saturation.

4 Copy the entry in the Hex box.

5 Paste the entry into your CSS style rule or wherever you want to use it.

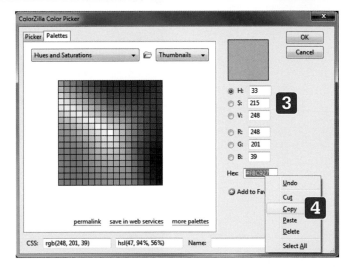

HOT TIP: Decrease the saturation for background colours, but increase it for foreground colours, including text.

WHAT DOES THIS MEAN?

Colour saturation: a measure of a colour's purity. The more saturated the colour is, the more intense it appears. The less saturated it is, the more washed out it looks – it becomes a dingy grey.

Hue, saturation and value: the three properties of colour. Hue is the colour itself, saturation the purity of the colour and value the lightness or darkness of a colour.

Change a colour's value

A colour's value is its lightness or darkness. The higher a colour's value, the lighter it is. You can use different values of the same colour to make objects on a page more or less prominent.

1 Run Firefox and choose the colour you want to adjust.

2 Open the ColorZilla menu and click Palette Browser.

3 Increase or decrease the colour's value.

4 Copy the entry in the Hex box.

5 Paste the entry into your CSS style rule or wherever you want to use it.

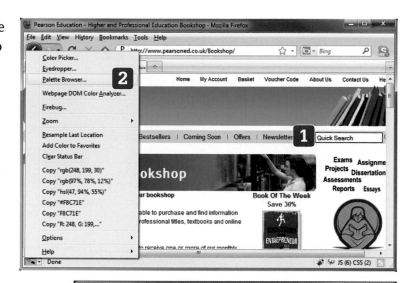

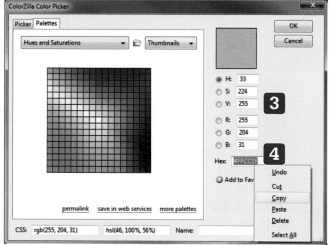

? DID YOU KNOW?

Colour value is often referred to as *luminance*.

WHAT DOES THIS MEAN?

Colour value: the lightness or darkness of a colour.

? DID YOU KNOW?

Increasing colour value creates a tint. At its highest value, every colour is white. Decreasing colour value creates a shade. At its lowest value, every colour is black.

Translate colours into codes

You may encounter colour specifications as RGB (red, green, blue) values rather than hex codes. In these situations, you can use ColorZilla to identify a colour's hex code.

1 In Firefox, open the ColorZilla menu and click Color Picker.

2 Type the RGB values into the R, G and B boxes.

3 Copy the entry in the Hex box.

4 Paste the entry into your CSS style rule or wherever you want to use it.

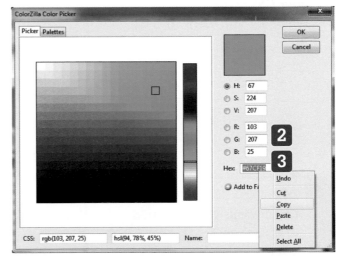

ALERT: RGB values range from 0 to 255.

DID YOU KNOW?
Setting R, G and B to the maximum of 255 produces white. Setting them to the minimum of 0 produces black.

DID YOU KNOW?
All colours in Web design are a combination of red, green and blue.

6 Choose a theme

Introduction

After installing a content management system (CMS) and adjusting a few basic settings, the next step is to choose and install a theme.

A theme is essentially a collection of styles that format your site from the header to the footer and everything in between. Your chosen theme controls the colours, fonts, font sizes, background, column width, and so on. Choosing a theme is not all about looks, though. Yes, a theme does control the overall appearance of a site, but it may also contribute to how functional and customisable your site is and its performance.

This chapter will show you how to find free and premium themes, decide which is a good theme, based on several criteria, and then download, install and activate a theme to put it in control of your site. You will perform several of the tasks from WordPress, so you will need to be logged in to it, as explained in Chapter 4.

Find free themes

Plenty of free themes are available for WordPress and you can find many of them without having to leave it.

1 In WordPress, open the Appearance menu and click Themes.

2 Click Install Themes.

3 Click one of the links near the top to browse the collection.

4 Search for a theme or filter themes by feature.

5 Browse the results.

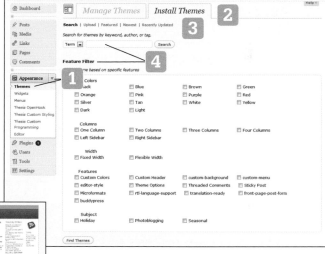

HOT TIP: You can search or browse a collection of more than 1000 free themes at http://wordpress.org/extend/themes.

HOT TIP: If you find a theme you like at wordpress.org, search for it in WordPress as then it will be easy to install.

Find premium themes

Premium themes may provide you with a more professional-looking site, along with additional features that make customising your site easier than can be the case with free ones. These themes are not free, however.

1 Go to http://wordpress.org/extend/themes and click Commercial.

2 Click a theme collection.

3 Browse the collection.

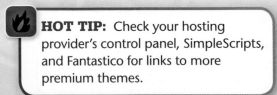

HOT TIP: Check your hosting provider's control panel, SimpleScripts, and Fantastico for links to more premium themes.

? DID YOU KNOW?
On most premium theme sites, you can pay by credit card or via a PayPal account.

Choose a theme's appearance

Appearance is the first consideration when deciding on a theme. You want to make sure that you like the colour scheme, fonts, header area and navigation details.

1 Make sure that the colour scheme is a good match for your site's purpose.

2 Check the height, width and design of the header area.

3 Be sure that the navigation controls are intuitive.

4 Check that the font styles and sizes suit your tastes.

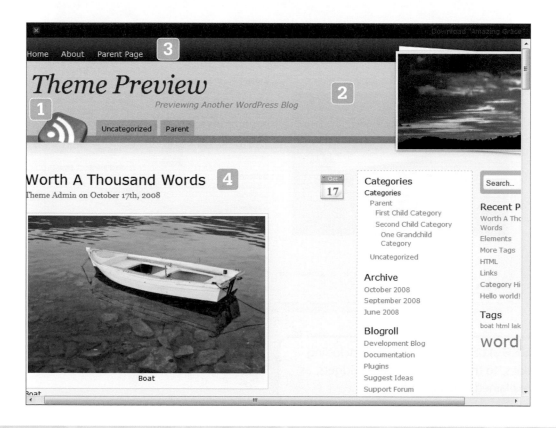

HOT TIP: Many premium themes enable you to switch colour schemes – simply select the desired colour or colour combination.

SEE ALSO: The theme does not need to be completely perfect – you can configure it by editing its CSS style sheet, as explained in Chapter 11.

Choose number of columns

One of the most important choices to make when selecting a theme is the number of columns it has, because this is a feature that is more difficult to adjust later.

 Make sure that the theme has the number of columns you need.

 Make sure the sidebar is where you want it – to the left or right.

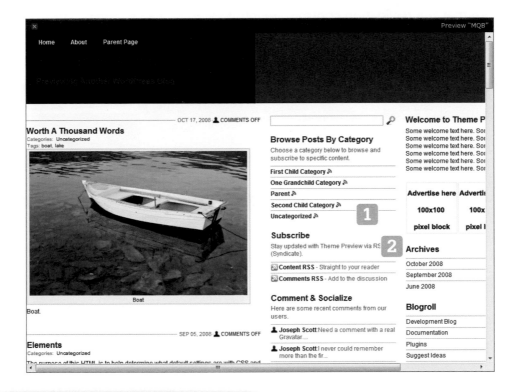

SEE ALSO: You add items, including links, to the sidebar by using widgets, as explained in Chapter 8.

? **DID YOU KNOW?**

A website typically positions the sidebar on the left because navigation is key. A blog, however, usually positions the most current posts on the left with the sidebar on the right.

HOT TIP: A three-column layout provides space for navigation, content and an extra column for whatever else you want to include.

Choose column widths

The width of each column is an important consideration, but it is something that you can easily adjust later. You want enough room for your featured content, along with a well-balanced page.

1 Gauge the amount of space you will need for your content, including photos.

2 Make sure that the page appears balanced.

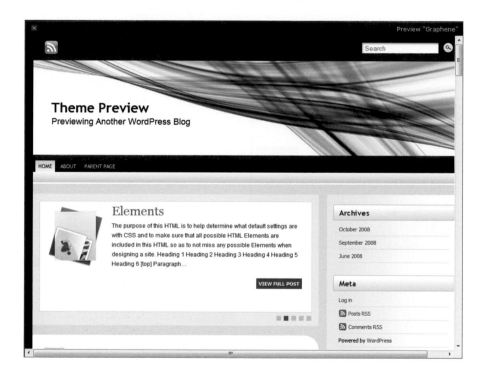

Choose fixed or flex width

You can choose from fixed-, flexible- or liquid-width themes. The steps below demonstrate the differences between these options.

1 A fixed-width theme maintains its width as display space changes.

2 A flexible-width theme adjusts column widths to accommodate more or less display space as required.

3 A liquid-width theme is flexible, but also adjusts font sizes to fit available space.

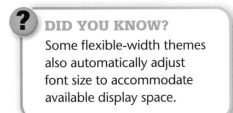

DID YOU KNOW?

Some flexible-width themes also automatically adjust font size to accommodate available display space.

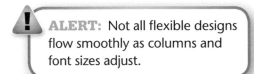

ALERT: Not all flexible designs flow smoothly as columns and font sizes adjust.

WHAT DOES THIS MEAN?

Fixed width: page and columns maintain width regardless of display space or font size.

Flexible width: page and column widths adjust to accommodate display space and font size.

Liquid width: they are flexible, but font size also adjusts to accommodate available space.

Choose functionality

Themes may vary in terms of how well they support the latest version of WordPress. Some may not give you access to the latest WordPress features and functionality.

1 At http://wordpress.org/extend/themes, click a theme you may want to use.

2 Click the Theme Homepage link.

3 Make sure the theme supports the latest version of WordPress.

4 Make sure the theme is widget-ready.

ALERT: The information that developers provide for their themes varies significantly.

Description

Wordpress Constructor Theme, it's many-in-one theme:

- six sidebar positions and three layouts (you can create new is easy)
- configured colors
- configured fonts
- configured footer text
- widgets ready (many sidebars)
- post thumbnails (Wordpress 2.9+)
- navigation menu (Wordpress 3.0+)

HOT TIP: Look for a theme that supports custom headers and other customisation features.

DID YOU KNOW? In addition to supporting WordPress functionality, many themes, especially premium themes, add functionality.

Check theme reviews

Perhaps the most valuable information you can obtain about a theme is from rankings and reviews by people who have actually used the theme. The steps below show how to check rankings and reviews in WordPress' themes gallery.

1 At http://wordpress.org/extend/themes, click a theme you may want to use.

2 Check the average rating and the number of ratings posted.

3 Click See what others are saying … to read additional comments and any warnings.

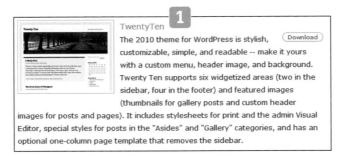

HOT TIP: Click the Stats tab above the theme's description to see the number of times the theme has been downloaded.

HOT TIP: If a theme has no rating or review, search for the theme by name, followed by 'wordpress' and you'll be likely to find comments from people who have used it.

Install a theme from within WordPress

The easiest way to install a theme is from within WordPress. The steps given below walk you through the process.

1 In WordPress, open the Appearance menu and click Themes.

2 Click Install Themes.

3 Click Install below the theme you want to install.

4 Click Install Now.

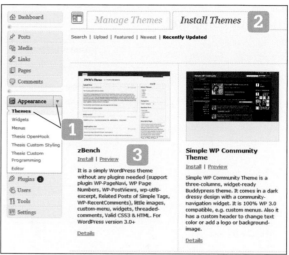

HOT TIP: Click Manage Themes to access your installed themes. From here, you can delete themes you no longer want.

SEE ALSO: If the theme you want is not accessible from WordPress, you must download it and then upload it to your Web server. See the following two sections for details. Also, after installing a theme, you must activate it to apply its styles to your site. See Activate a theme at the end of this chapter.

Download a theme

If you find a free or premium theme you want to use and cannot access it in WordPress, you must download the theme and then upload it to your Web server.

1 Click the link for downloading the theme.

2 Save the theme to a folder on your computer.

3 Double-click the compressed file and extract its contents to a separate folder on your computer.

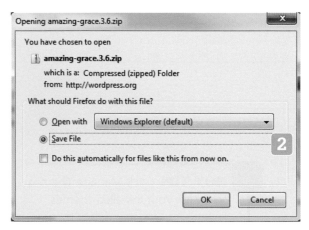

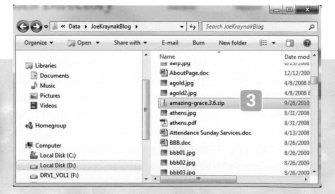

Upload a theme

To make a theme accessible from WordPress, you must upload the theme to the 'wp-content/themes' directory of the folder in which you installed WordPress.

1 Run your FTP client and change to the 'wp-content/themes' directory on the server.

2 Click the theme folder you extracted in the previous section on your computer.

3 Click the Upload button (top arrow).

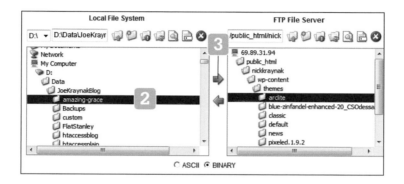

4 Wait until the upload has been completed.

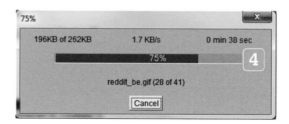

ALERT: The steps you need to take vary depending on the theme. Check the theme's home page or readme.txt file for specific installation instructions.

SEE ALSO: Chapter 3 for details on uploading files via FTP.

Activate a theme

After uploading a theme, you must activate it from within WordPress. As soon as you activate the theme, WordPress applies its formatting to all pages that comprise your site.

1 In WordPress, open the Appearance menu and click Themes.

2 In the list of Available Themes, click the Activate link below the theme you want to use.

3 Click the site's title to check out the new design.

4 Your browser then displays the site with this newly activated theme.

 HOT TIP: Installing a theme may add menus or options to your WordPress installation. Check the menus for any new features.

 DID YOU KNOW?
To deactivate the current theme, simply activate a different one.

7 Customise the header

Introduction

One of the most prominent features of any website or blog is its header. Visit a site's home page and its header is the first thing that greets you. Click through the pages on the site and the header is there, wherever you go. A quality header can give your site a recognisable presence, so make it as engaging and attractive as possible. This chapter will show you how.

Here you'll discover what a header is, explore your header options and learn a couple of easy ways to customise it. As you work your way through the section 'Identify the header's dimensions' and those that follow, you'll be led through the process of creating a custom header image for your site.

To perform many of the steps in this chapter, you must be logged in to WordPress. See Chapter 4 for login instructions. Also keep in mind that header customisation varies from theme to theme, so option names and locations may be differ from what is shown.

Know your header options

The header is the band that appears at the top of a page, typically on every page of a website or blog. It may consist of text only, text plus an image or one big image. It may also have built-in navigation.

1 Place text in the header area.

2 Add a background colour.

3 Use an image as the header.

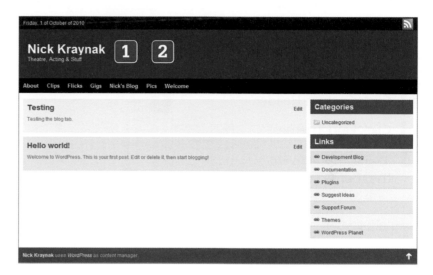

> ⚠ **ALERT:** Clicking a header typically takes a user back to the site's home page.

WHAT DOES THIS MEAN?

Header: the top of a Web page, which typically contains the site's title and tagline.

❓ DID YOU KNOW?

The theme determines the default header, but you can change it, as shown in this chapter.

Install a custom header theme

Some WordPress themes feature header customisation from the WordPress Dashboard, which makes the task of customising the header much easier.

1 In WordPress, open the Appearance menu and click Themes.

2 Click Install Themes.

3 Click Custom Header.

4 Click Find Themes.

5 Install and activate the theme you want.

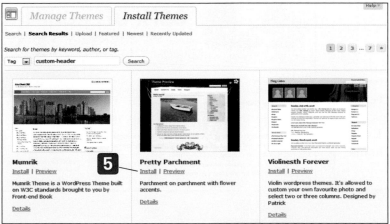

? DID YOU KNOW?

If you choose something other than a custom header theme, you can still customise it, but how you do this is shown later in this chapter.

▶ SEE ALSO: Chapter 6 for more on selecting and installing a WordPress theme.

Configure the header in a custom header theme

Many themes, including the WordPress default theme, feature options for customising the header without having to edit the theme's files.

1. Click the option for customising the header in the Appearance menu.

2. Enter your preferences.

3. Click Save Changes.

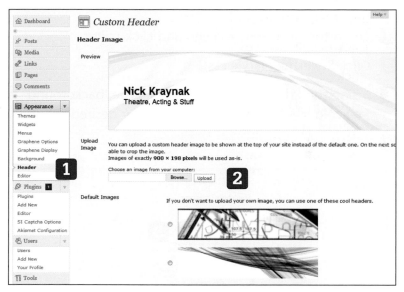

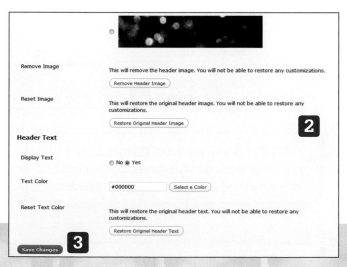

ALERT: The header option may be on a different menu, and the options vary from theme to theme.

? DID YOU KNOW?
In some themes, controls enable you to add a logo or choose a header image to upload.

Add background shading to a text-based header

If the theme you are using has a text-based header (no image) and no option for customising it, you can change or add background shading to give it some colour. You do this by editing the theme's header style in its style sheet.

1 Open the Appearance menu and click Editor.

2 Click Stylesheet (style.css).

3 Inside the '#header' style brackets, type 'background: #hexcolour', replacing 'hexcolour' with the hex code for your desired colour.

4 Click Update File.

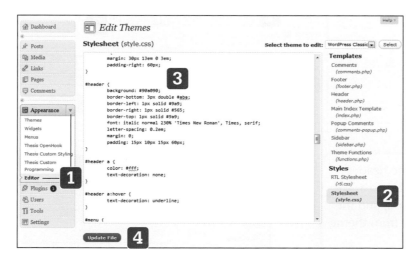

ALERT: Some premium themes do not enable you to edit stylesheets, but feature other methods for customising the header.

ALERT: If your theme has a custom header option, use it, as explained in the previous section, instead of editing the stylesheet.

SEE ALSO: Chapter 11 for details on editing stylesheets and Chapter 5 for more on colour hex codes.

Identify the header's dimensions

This and the remaining sections in this chapter show you how to replace a theme's existing header image with a new one of the same dimensions. The first step is to determine the dimensions of the existing image.

1 In WordPress, open the Appearance menu and click Editor.

2 Click Stylesheet (style.css).

3 Scroll down to the '#header' selector and note the height and width properties.

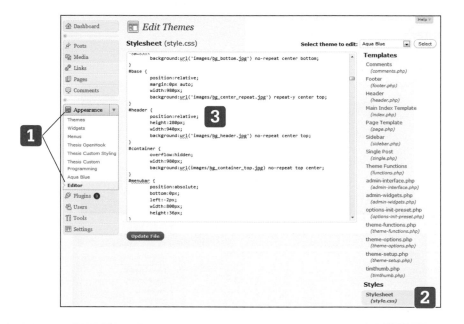

ALERT: The focus here is on themes that include a single header image. In some themes, a header can consist of two or more images.

WHAT DOES THIS MEAN?

Selector: the part of a CSS style rule that targets an element for formatting.

HOT TIP: In the Mozilla Firefox Web browser, right-click the header image and click View Image Info to obtain the image's dimensions. You may need to click View Background Image first. (This does not work if the image is a link.)

Choose a header image

To create a custom header, start by creating or downloading a suitable header image. Find out below how to download free header art from Digital Westex.

1 Go to www.digitalwestex.com/gallery and click the dimensions that most nearly match those of the existing header image.

2 Click the header image you want.

3 Click the image to view it full size.

4 Right-click the image and save it to your computer.

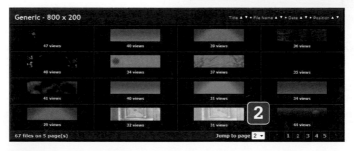

🔥 **HOT TIP:** If you can't find a match, download a larger image and then crop it.

🔥 **HOT TIP:** For more header art, search the Web for 'wordpress header art'.

Upload your header image

To liven up your header art, upload it into a banner application, such as BannerFans, then add text and special effects. Learn below how to upload your image.

1 Go to http://bannerfans.com and click I want to upload my own image.

2 Click Browse and choose the header art image on your computer.

3 Click Update my banner.

4 BannerFans displays the image.

Add text

After uploading your header art, edit the placeholder text on the banner to add your site's title and tagline.

1 Click the Text & Fonts tab.

2 Edit the Line 1 and Line 2 entries to add your site's title and tagline.

3 Select the Font face, font size, colour and rotation for the text.

4 Click Update my banner.

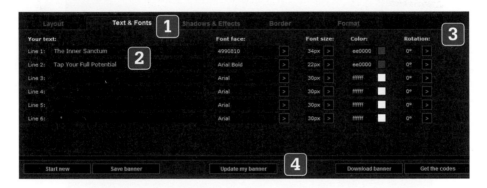

5 Drag the text to position it on the image.

? DID YOU KNOW?

The Rotation option enables you to present the text at an angle, up or down.

🔥 HOT TIP: You can add more text to the header by typing it in the Line 3–6 boxes.

Add shadows and effects

Adding a shadow and outline to text makes it appear well-defined and three-dimensional.

1 Click the Shadows & Effects tab.

2 Enter your preferences for shadow position, distance, colour, text opacity, text outline and outline colour.

3 Click Update my banner.

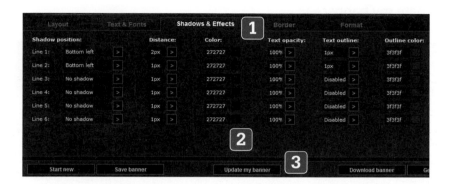

4 Check the results of your changes.

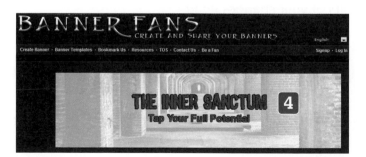

! **ALERT:** Avoid the temptation to offset the shadow too much. Minor adjustments often lead to major improvements.

? **DID YOU KNOW?**
In most cases, the shadow position setting should be the same for all the lines, so that all the light appears to be coming from the same direction.

Add a border

A border around the header image clearly defines its edges and provides you with another way to add colour to your site.

1 Click the Border tab.

2 Select the desired border style.

3 Enter additional preferences.

4 Click Update my banner.

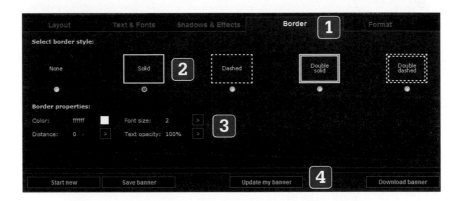

5 Check the results of your changes.

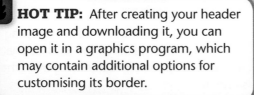

HOT TIP: After creating your header image and downloading it, you can open it in a graphics program, which may contain additional options for customising its border.

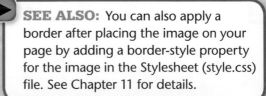

SEE ALSO: You can also apply a border after placing the image on your page by adding a border-style property for the image in the Stylesheet (style.css) file. See Chapter 11 for details.

Download your banner

When your banner has been completed, download it to your computer. Find out below how to specify your preferred file format and then download the file.

1 Click the Format tab.

2 Click the desired format option.

3 Click the Download banner button.

4 Save the banner file to a folder on your computer.

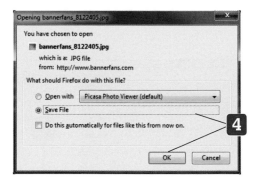

 HOT TIP: To save your banner so you can edit it later, click the Save banner button and then sign up for a login name and password.

? DID YOU KNOW?
Although the .PNG format is a higher quality, .JPG is sufficient and smaller and loads faster.

Upload your banner to your site

To use your banner, it must be on the Web and the best place to store it is in your theme's 'images' folder.

1 In your FTP client, change to your theme's 'images' folder.

2 Select the header image you created.

3 Click the Upload button (top arrow).

4 Wait until the upload has been completed.

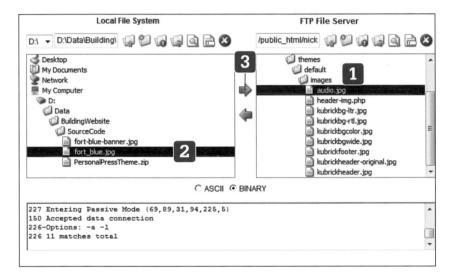

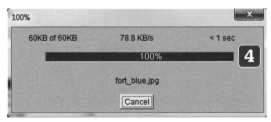

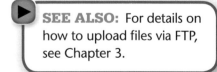

SEE ALSO: For details on how to upload files via FTP, see Chapter 3.

 HOT TIP: To replace an existing header image, delete the old image and give your new image the same filename.

HOT TIP: If you are using a custom header theme, you may be able to use the theme's controls from inside WordPress to upload the banner.

Add the banner to your theme

If you replaced an existing header image with a new one of the same name, you can skip this step. Otherwise, you must add a tag or style to your theme to include the header image.

1. In WordPress, open the Appearance menu and click Editor.

2. Open the Header (header.php) file.

3. Add the tags from the '<a' block as shown, replacing the highlighted text with the URL of your header image.

4. Open the Stylesheet (style.css) file.

5. Edit the '#header' style to change the dimensions, if necessary.

6. Delete the style property responsible for inserting the previous header image, if present.

7. Click Update File.

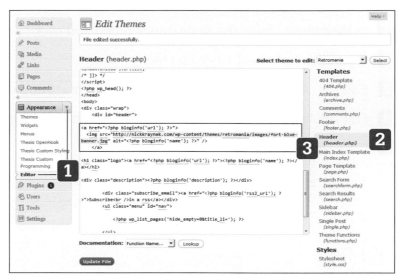

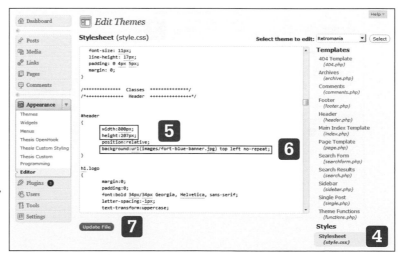

ALERT: Themes differ from one another in terms of how they handle the header. Look for header styles and tags in both the theme's Header and Stylesheet files.

ALERT: After changing the header image, you may need to make additional style changes to blend it in with the rest of the design. See Chapter 11 for more on styles.

Hide site title and tagline

If you add a header image that contains text, you may end up with the text that is part of the image overlaid by the title and tagline from WordPress' general settings! You can hide this text by moving it off the screen.

1 In WordPress, open the Appearance menu and click Editor.

2 Open the Stylesheet (style.css) file.

3 Edit the '#logo' style to give it a left margin of -1000px.

4 Edit the '#tagline' style to give it a left margin of -1000px.

5 Click Update File.

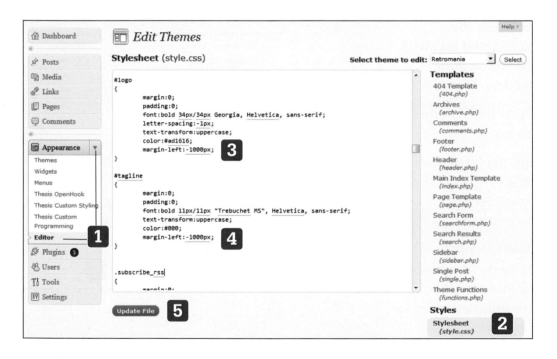

ALERT: You can hide text by adding the property 'display:none;' to its style, but this may cause search engines to ignore it.

8 Configure your site with widgets

Introduction

Most themes have one to three sidebars. A sidebar is a narrow column that appears to the left or right of the content area. WordPress Widgets (WPWs) are modules that you can add to, remove from and arrange within your site's sidebar(s) to enhance navigation and add functionality. For example, WordPress features widgets for adding a calendar of your site's posts, a list of pages or categories, search box, links to favourite sites and so on.

This chapter shows you how to 'widgetise' (accessorise) your site and even create your own custom widget. Each section assumes that you are using a theme with at least one sidebar and logged in to WordPress (see Chapter 4 for details about logging in to WordPress).

Add widgets to your site

WordPress includes a collection of widgets you can add to any sidebar simply by dragging and dropping them into the sidebar of your choice.

1 Open the Appearance menu and click Widgets.

2 Expand the destination sidebar box.

3 Drag the widget to the sidebar and drop it in place.

> **?** **DID YOU KNOW?**
> A theme may have two sidebars and allow you to use one or both of them.

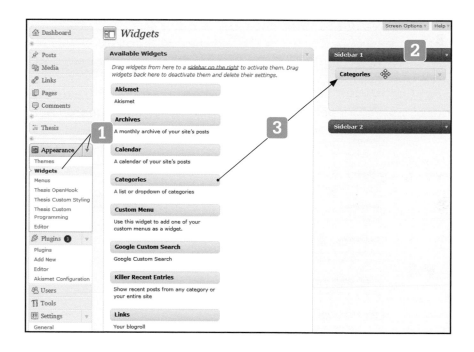

> **!** **ALERT:** If you have difficulty working with widgets – such as a widget not appearing where you dropped it – try a different Web browser.

> **▶** **SEE ALSO:** After dropping a widget into a sidebar box, the widget may expand and prompt you to enter settings. The next section shows you how to enter these.

Enter widget settings

After you drop a widget into a sidebar box, it typically expands as a way to prompt you to enter information – such as a name for the widget – or change settings to customise the way that it functions.

1 Expand the widget, if necessary.

2 Type the requested entry.

3 Select your preferences.

4 Click Save.

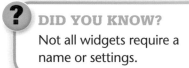

Create a text widget

The WordPress Text widget is more than its name implies. You can use it to add text to a sidebar, but you can also use it to add images or custom code.

1 Expand the text widget, if necessary.

2 Type a title, if desired.

3 Enter your text.

4 You may include HTML to format text or insert elements, including images.

5 Click Save.

HOT TIP: For the RSS Feed widget, you need the address of the feed. Your site address followed by '/feed' should work – www.yoursite.co.uk/feed, for example.

WHAT DOES THIS MEAN?

RSS feed: a summary of content on your site that visitors can subscribe to.

SEE ALSO: To format text or add elements, such as images, via a text widget, you need to know HTML. See Chapter 10 for details. Note, too, that the Stylesheet (styles.css) file controls the appearance of the sidebar title. See Chapter 11 for details on editing the styles in this file.

Rearrange widgets

You may move widgets around, arranging them however you like in your sidebar(s). Here's how.

1 Drag a widget up or down.

2 Drop it in place.

HOT TIP: You can edit the contents of a widget at any time. Simply click the arrow to the right of the widget's bar to expand it, then enter your changes.

 DID YOU KNOW?

As you drag a widget to a new location, a dotted rule box appears, indicating where the widget will be placed when you release the mouse button.

DID YOU KNOW?

WordPress automatically updates your site whenever you change the contents inside one of the sidebar boxes.

Remove widgets

You can easily remove widgets from a sidebar by simply dragging and dropping them into the Available Widgets or Inactive Widgets area.

1 Drag the widget from the sidebar.

2 Drop the widget in the Available Widgets area to remove it and its settings.

3 Drop the widget in the Inactive Widgets area to remove it but save its settings.

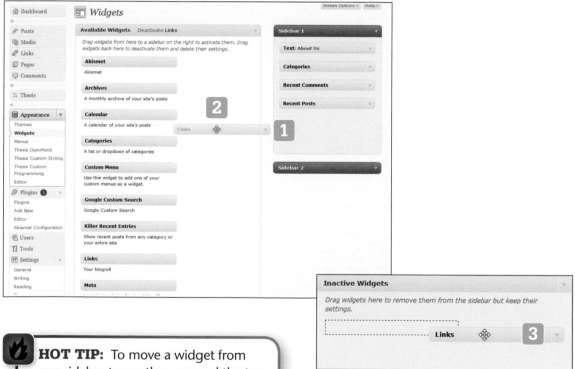

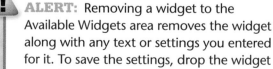

HOT TIP: To move a widget from one sidebar to another, expand the two sidebar boxes, then drag and drop the widget from one box to the other.

ALERT: Removing a widget to the Available Widgets area removes the widget along with any text or settings you entered for it. To save the settings, drop the widget in to the Inactive Widgets area.

DID YOU KNOW?
You can add an inactive widget back to the sidebar by dragging it from the Inactive Widgets area and dropping it in the sidebar.

Find and install more widgets

Although WordPress comes complete with its own collection of widgets, you can find plenty more. Here, I'll show you where to look and how to obtain more information about a particular widget.

1 Go to http://codex.wordpress.org/WordPress_Widgets and scroll down the page to the heading 'List of Widgets'.

2 Click a widget to find out more about it, including how to install it.

ALERT: If a widget is packaged in a compressed .zip file, you will need to extract the widget from the .zip file – unzip it – before installing it.

SEE ALSO: You can also find and install widgets by doing a plugin search in WordPress. For details on performing a plugin search, see Chapter 9.

3 Click the Download button to save the widget.

4 Install the widget, following the instructions you found out about in Step 2.

 DID YOU KNOW?

Many developers package their widgets in plugins, so you can install a plugin that adds widgets to your WordPress installation.

WHAT DOES THIS MEAN?

Widget: a modular mini application that makes it easy to accessorise a website, blog or page.

9 Accessorise your site with plugins

Introduction

Plugins are modules that add features and functionality to WordPress. I like to think of them as accessories. You can use plugins to improve your site's performance, add a contact form, track traffic on your site, enable visitors to easily tweet about content, provide enhanced tools for managing your site and just about anything else you can imagine.

This chapter enables you to tap the power of plugins. Here, I share my list of top 10 plugins, show you how to find them and check user reviews, install and configure plugins and use a few popular ones. After witnessing the power of plugins and how easy they are to install, you will no doubt find your own favourites.

Many of the steps in this chapter require that you are logged in to WordPress. See Chapter 4 for more about logging in to WordPress.

Explore 10 valuable plugins

Nearly everyone who has a WordPress site has a list of 5–10 favourite plugins. Here's my list, along with instructions on how to find out more information about them.

1 Check out my list of top 10 plugins.

2 Open the Plugins menu and click Add New.

3 Search for a plugin by name.

4 Check the plugin's rating and description.

 HOT TIP: BuddyPress is a popular plugin for adding a social networking area to your site.

Favourite WordPress Plugins

- ✓ AddToAny: Share/Bookmark/Email Button
- ✓ Askimet
- ✓ Dagon Design Form Mailer **1**
- ✓ Google XML Sitemaps
- ✓ HeadSpace 2: WordPress SEO Made Simple
- ✓ NextGEN Photo Gallery
- ✓ Nofollow Case by Case
- ✓ SI CAPTCHA Anti-Spam
- ✓ W3 Total Cache
- ✓ WPtouch iPhone Theme

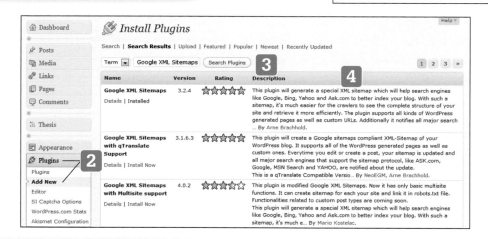

 SEE ALSO: Many plugins are in the widget category. For more on widgets, see Chapter 8.

WHAT DOES THIS MEAN?

Plugin: a modular application that adds features and functionality to a host application.

 HOT TIP: Find out what others think. Search the Web for 'best wordpress plugins' and you are sure to find other WordPress users' top 10, 20 or 30 favourite plugin lists.

Find free plugins

You can browse a collection of plugins or search for specific plugins from within WordPress. This makes installing a plugin, once you find one you want, much easier than other options.

1 Open the Plugins menu and click Add New.

2 Browse or search for the plugin you need.

3 Check the plugin's rating and description.

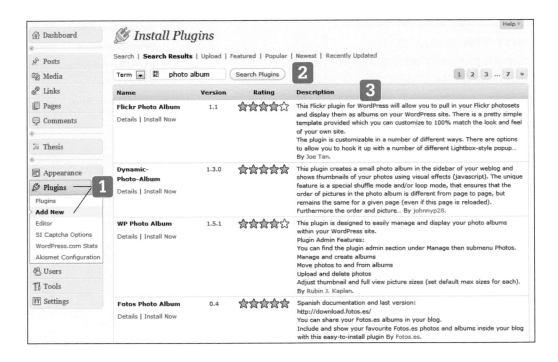

HOT TIP: You can also find free plugins at http://wordpress.org/extend/plugins.

Investigate a plugin's details

Before installing a plugin, check its ratings, reviews, number of downloads and other pertinent information.

1 Display the entry for the plugin you want to check.

2 Click Details.

3 Read the description.

4 Check the average rating.

5 Check how many times it has been downloaded.

6 Make sure the plugin is compatible with your version of WordPress.

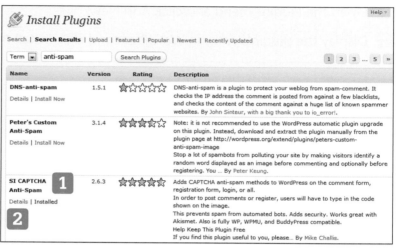

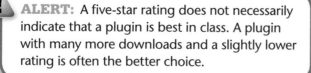

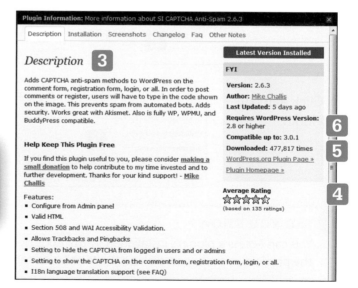

> 🔥 **HOT TIP:** You can also find plugin ratings and reviews at http://wordpress.org/extend/plugins.

> ⚠️ **ALERT:** A five-star rating does not necessarily indicate that a plugin is best in class. A plugin with many more downloads and a slightly lower rating is often the better choice.

> ❓ **DID YOU KNOW?**
> Scroll to the bottom of any WordPress window and you can see the WordPress version number in the lower right-hand corner.

Install a plugin

Installing a plugin is typically a very easy operation, especially if you install it from within WordPress. Here is what you need to do.

1 Open the Plugins menu and click Add New.

2 Display the plugin's entry in WordPress and click Install Now.

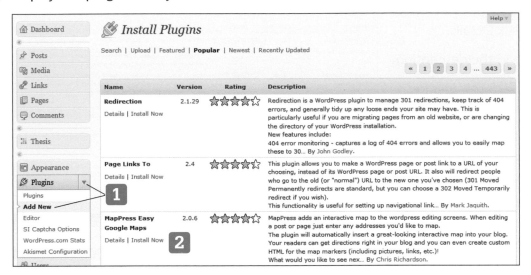

3 Click Activate Plugin.

? DID YOU KNOW?
You can access a plugin's installation instructions by pulling up its details, as explained in the previous section, and clicking the Installation tab.

! ALERT: Most plugins start performing their jobs immediately, but you may need to take additional steps to configure others. Check the plugin's installation instructions for details.

▶ SEE ALSO: Some plugins need to be installed manually. You download a .zip file, extract the folder it contains, then upload it to the wp-content/plugins folder. See Chapter 3 for details on uploading files and folders.

Change plugin settings

When you install a plugin, it often adds a menu to the WordPress Dashboard or an option to an existing menu, such as Settings or Plugins. You can then use the option or menu to configure the plugin's settings.

1 Look for new menus or options, especially on the Settings menu.

2 Click the plugin's customisation option.

3 Use the resulting control panel to enter your preferences.

4 Save your changes.

ALERT: Not all plugins add options to the WordPress Dashboard.

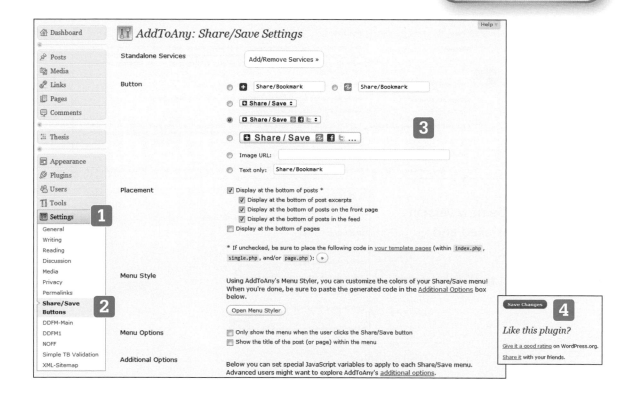

ALERT: In your list of installed plugins, you will see an Edit link for each plugin. This is usually not what you click to customise a plugin's operation, but if you cannot find settings anywhere else, try clicking the Edit link.

DID YOU KNOW? Some plugins are very complex, offering dozens of configuration options.

Update plugins

Plugin developers often modify their plugins and release new versions. If there is a newer version of one of your plugins WordPress will display a message below it in the list of installed plugins, notifying you. You should install the most recent version.

1 Open the Plugins menu and click Plugins.

2 Click 'upgrade automatically' at the end of the message.

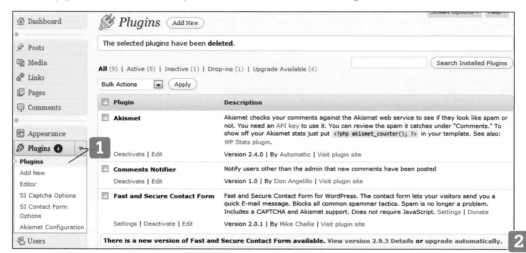

3 Wait until the new version has been installed and reactivated.

4 Click Return to Plugins page.

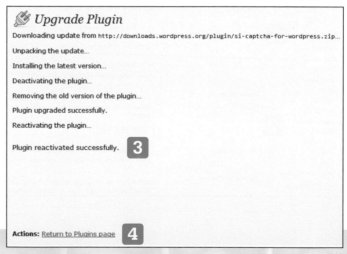

 ALERT: If you manually installed the plugin by uploading it via FTP, you will probably need to upgrade it by following the same steps.

 HOT TIP: When one or more plugins have newer versions, WordPress displays a dark circle on the Plugins menu with the number of plugins that are out of date, as shown in the screenshot.

Reduce spam with Askimet

Askimet checks any comments posted on your site against its database of known spammers, enabling you to preview suspicious comments before approving them. Askimet is installed in WordPress by default. All you need to do is activate it and enter an API key for it.

1 Activate Askimet.

2 Open the Plugins menu and click Askimet Configuration.

3 Type your Askimet API Key in the API Key box.

4 Click Update options.

> **ALERT:** Before activating Askimet, go to http://akismet.com/get to obtain your API key. It's free for personal use and very affordable for business use.

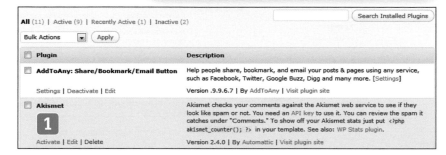

> **? DID YOU KNOW?**
>
> Askimet is installed in WordPress by default. All you need to do is activate it and enter an API key for it.

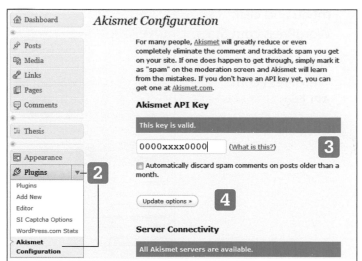

WHAT DOES THIS MEAN?

Spam: unwanted and, typically, undesirable comments, often posted as advertisements or to link your site to another to make that site seem more important to search engines.

? DID YOU KNOW?

To review comments posted on your site, click Comments. The Spam link at the top lets you view comments that Askimet has identified as possible spam.

Track your site's statistics

To see who is visiting your site and which of your pages and posts are most popular, install an analytics plugin such as WordPress.com Stats.

1 Install and activate WordPress.com Stats.

2 Open the Plugins menu and click WordPress.com Stats.

3 Enter your WordPress.com API key.

4 Click Save.

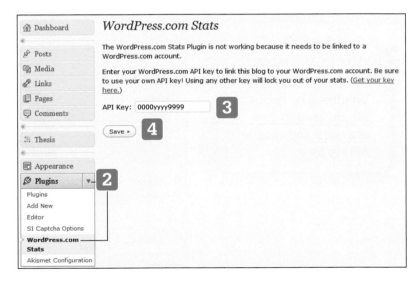

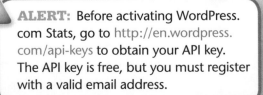

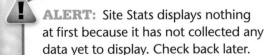

! ALERT: Before activating WordPress.com Stats, go to http://en.wordpress.com/api-keys to obtain your API key. The API key is free, but you must register with a valid email address.

! ALERT: Site Stats displays nothing at first because it has not collected any data yet to display. Check back later.

5 Open the Dashboard menu and click Site Stats.

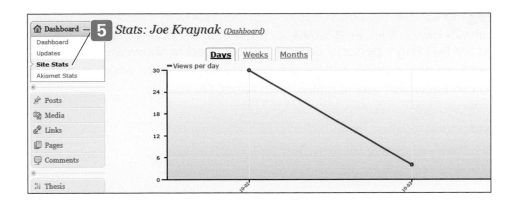

ALERT: Don't overdo it with plugins – having too many may negatively affect your site's performance. See Chapter 14 for more on performance issues.

? DID YOU KNOW?
Most plugins are free, but developers often ask for donations.

▶ SEE ALSO: Install a plugin section earlier in this chapter.

Add a photo or slideshow gallery

Whether you are building a personal or family site or need to showcase products or services, a photo or slideshow gallery can significantly enhance what your site is offering. You can easily add such a gallery with NextGEN Gallery.

1 Install and activate NextGEN Gallery.

2 Open the Gallery menu and click Add Gallery/ Images.

3 Type a name for the gallery

4 Click Add gallery.

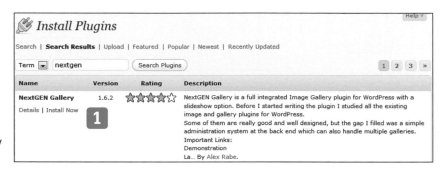

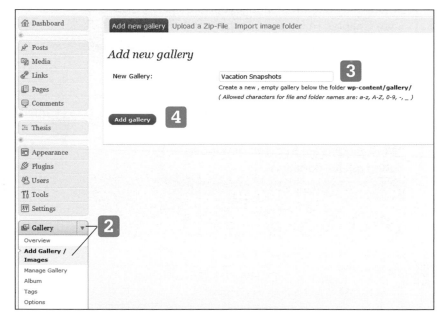

HOT TIP: Edit thumbnails via the Gallery Manager. Click Manage Gallery, click the gallery and make your adjustments to the thumbnails.

DID YOU KNOW?

The steps given here are merely to get you started with NextGEN Gallery – explore the options on the Gallery menu to discover the many other possibilities.

5 Browse and upload images to the gallery from your computer.

6 Create a new post or page for the gallery.

7 Click Add NextGEN Gallery.

8 Select the desired gallery and options.

9 Click Insert.

10 Publish the page or post.

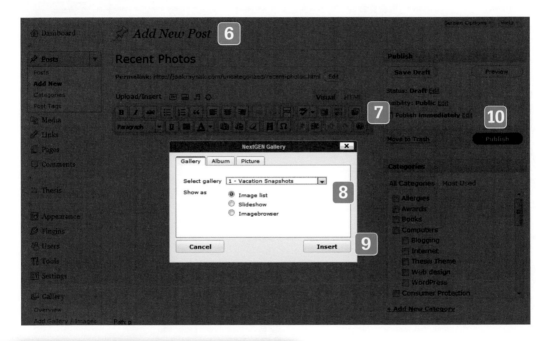

HOT TIP: Plugins are available that add functionality to NextGEN Gallery.

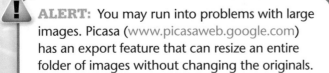

ALERT: You may run into problems with large images. Picasa (www.picasaweb.google.com) has an export feature that can resize an entire folder of images without changing the originals.

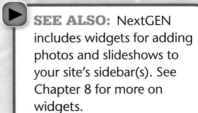

SEE ALSO: NextGEN includes widgets for adding photos and slideshows to your site's sidebar(s). See Chapter 8 for more on widgets.

Add social bookmarks

When you post blog entries on your site, you usually want people to know about it. To help spread the word, include social bookmarks icons so that visitors can click to share your content on Facebook, Twitter, and other social networking sites.

1 Install and activate AddToAny: Share/Bookmark/Email Button.

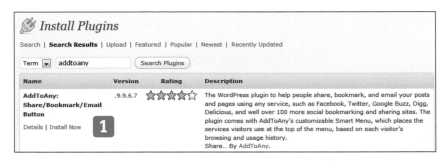

2 Open the Settings menu and click Share/Save Buttons.

3 Enter your Preferences.

4 Click Save Changes.

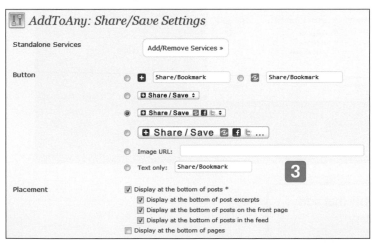

WHAT DOES THIS MEAN?

Social networking: the act of sharing interests and information in an online community, such as on Facebook.

HOT TIP: Click Add/Remove Services at the top of the Share/Save Settings screen to add or remove social networking services and/or rearrange them on the menu.

Troubleshoot plugins

Many problems on WordPress sites can be traced back to a specific plugin. If you are experiencing problems on your site, try deactivating your plugins and then reactivating them one at a time. The steps below show you how to do this.

1 Open the Plugins menu and click Plugins.

2 Click the plugin's Deactivate link.

3 To reactivate the plugin, click its Activate link.

10 Add and format pages and posts with HTML

Introduction

Although your site design is important, on the Web, content is king. Visitors come and, more importantly, come back to your site because of its content. That is really where a CMS like WordPress shines. WordPress facilitates the process of placing content on the Web and modifying it.

Whether you are building a website or maintaining a blog, posting content to your site is as simple as logging in, clicking an option to create a new page or post, typing your content, then clicking the Publish button. In this chapter, you will discover just how easy it is.

Note that, to perform any of the tasks in this chapter, you must be logged in to WordPress. See Chapter 4 for details.

Create a new page

In WordPress, pages form the static content on your site. Most sites include a home page, welcoming visitors, an about page that provides general information about the site and a few other pages that vary from site to site.

1 Open the Pages menu and click Add New.

2 Type a title for your page.

3 Type the content you want to include.

4 Drag the corner of the window to make it larger.

SEE ALSO: To format your text, see Format a page or post in visual mode, next, and, to add images and videos to a post, see Chapter 13.

? DID YOU KNOW?
If you're managing a blog exclusively (with no pages), your site has only a blog that contains a running list of your posts.

HOT TIP: Under Page Attributes, you can choose a parent page. Then, the name of the new page will appear below it in your site's page navigation.

Create a new post

In WordPress, blog entries are called posts. They typically appear in reverse chronological order on the blog page – that is, with the most recent post at the top.

1 Open the Posts menu and click Add New.

2 Type a title for the post.

3 Type the content for your post.

4 Drag the corner of the window to make it larger.

5 Create or select a category for your post.

? DID YOU KNOW?
To manage categories, open the Posts menu and click Categories.

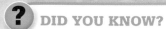

? DID YOU KNOW?
To create a category for a post, click the + Add New Category link in the Categories menu, type the name of the category, then click Add New Category.

HOT TIP: You do not need to complete a post or page right away. You can click Save Draft in the Publish menu, then come back later to complete it.

Add an e-mail contact form to your site

An e-mail contact form enables visitors to contact you via e-mail, but keeps your e-mail address hidden from spammers.

1 Install and activate the secure e-mail form plugin of your choice.

2 Click the option to edit the e-mail plugin's settings.

3 Enter your e-mail address and any additional preferences and save the settings.

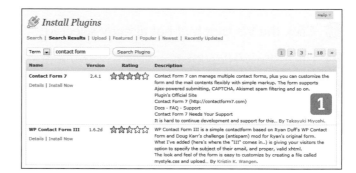

4 Create a WordPress page for the e-mail form.

5 Copy and paste or type the code required to display the form.

HOT TIP: I prefer Dagon Design's Form Mailer (DDFM), but you must install it manually. Visit www.dagondesign.com/articles/secure-form-mailer-plugin-for-wordpress for the plugin and installation instructions. Other e-mail contact form plugins are available for WordPress, but DDFM has a nice clean look and is simple to use.

ALERT: Test your contact form to make sure it is working by sending a message to yourself.

SEE ALSO: Chapter 9 for details on finding and installing plugins.

Format a page or post in visual mode

If you have experience of formatting documents in a word processing program, you know everything you need to know to format a page or post in visual mode. See the following steps just to make sure you know what you're doing!

1 Click the Visual tab, if not already selected.

2 Click Show/Hide Kitchen Sink to show more or fewer formatting options.

3 Select the text you want to format.

4 Click a button or select an option to apply the desired formatting.

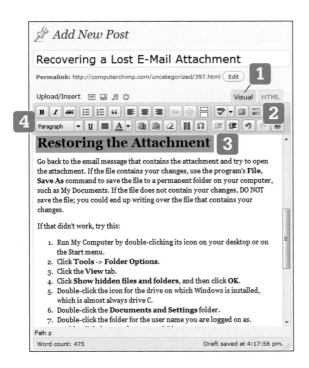

HOT TIP: Rest the mouse pointer on a button to view its name, which typically indicates what the button does.

? DID YOU KNOW?

The Insert More button inserts a line break wherever you want. Only content above the line appears in the list of posts, so visitors must click the post's title to view the rest.

HOT TIP: To give yourself more room to work, click the Toggle Fullscreen Mode button.

Display a page or post in HTML view

If you need to insert an HTML tag in your post (to include a YouTube video, for example), you must insert it in HTML view.

1 Create your post in Visual mode.

2 Click the HTML tag.

3 WordPress displays the HTML source code for your page or post.

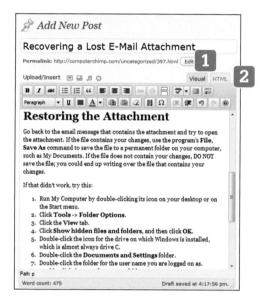

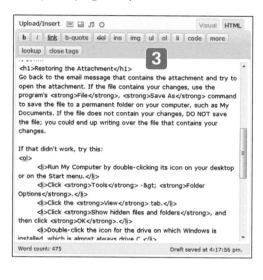

ALERT: If you see an HTML tag such as '<strong>' in Visual mode, you probably typed or pasted the tab in Visual mode by mistake. Cut the tag, change to HTML view and paste it back in place.

? DID YOU KNOW?
HTML view is great for troubleshooting formatting that does not appear as you want.

WHAT DOES THIS MEAN?

HTML: short for HyperText Markup Language, these tags are used to identify the elements that comprise a Web page.

► SEE ALSO: The next section, Explore essential HTML tags.

Explore essential HTML tags

With the help of WordPress's Visual mode, you can usually avoid HTML, but you should know some essential tags as they can come in handy, especially if you need to post a comment in response to a visitor's comment.

Table 10.1 HTML tags

Format	HTML tag
Paragraph	<p>Paragraph text</p>
Line break	
Bold	Bold
Italic	<i>Italic</i>
<u>Underline</u>	<u>Underline</u>
~~Strikethrough~~	<s>Strikethrough</s>
Big size	<big>Big size</big>
Small size	<small>Small size</small>
En dash, like –	&ndash;
Hyperlink	<a href='http://website.co.uk' >Link Text</a>
Image	<img src='http://website.co.uk/images/image.jpg' />
Unordered (bulleted) list	<ul>
• Item	<li>Item</li>
• Item	<li>Item</li>
• Item	<li>Item</li>
• Item	<li>Item</li>

SEE ALSO: For a complete list of HTML5 tags and more information about them, visit http://w3schools.com/html5/html5_reference.asp.

144

Format	HTML tag
End unordered list	</ul>
Ordered (numbered) List	<ol>
1 Step one	<li>Step one</li>
2 Step two	<li>Step two</li>
3 Step three	<li>Step three</li>
4 Step four	<li>Step four</li>
End unordered list	</ol>
Indented quote	<blockquote>Indented quote</blockquote>
Heading 1	<h1>Heading 1</h1>
Heading 2	<h1>Heading 2</h1>
Heading 3	<h1>Heading 3</h1>

 DID YOU KNOW?
Most HTML tags are paired – that is, they require an opening and closing tag. Others, such as the '<img />' tag, are unpaired, opening and closing themselves.

 ALERT: Formatting in Visual mode is usually better than HTML, because WordPress inserts the tags for you, eliminating the risk of typing errors.

Choose whether or not to allow comments

Unless you specify otherwise, all pages and posts will have a comment box at the end in which visitors can post comments on your content. You can choose to omit the comment box on individual pages and posts.

1 Scroll down the Add New Page or Add New Post screen to the Discussion options.

2 Click the Allow comments option to remove the tick and hide the comments box.

3 Click the Allow trackbacks and pingbacks on this page option to remove the tick and disallow trackbacks and pingbacks.

WHAT DOES THIS MEAN?

Trackback: an excerpt from a comment published on another blog in response to your post that includes a link back to the comment's point of origin.

Pingback: a link back to a comment in response to your post that appears on another site. (Similar to a trackback, but without the excerpt of the comment.)

Preview a page or post

Although Visual mode displays your formatted post or page, it does not display it in the context of your site's design. To see your content in context, preview it.

1 Click the Preview button.

2 Your browser will display the page or post in a separate window or tab.

3 Close the window or tab to return to WordPress.

ALERT: If your browser is set to block popups, it may not display the preview window, but you will probably see a button or bar you can click to enable the preview popup.

? DID YOU KNOW?

Preview is especially useful if your page or post contains images, because they may look quite different when you preview them.

Publish a page or post

When you have completed your page or post, publish it to place it on your site. By default, pages and posts are published immediately and are publicly accessible, but you can change these options prior to publishing.

1 Click the Publish button.

2 WordPress publishes the page or post and displays confirmation.

3 Click View post to double-check that it looks acceptable.

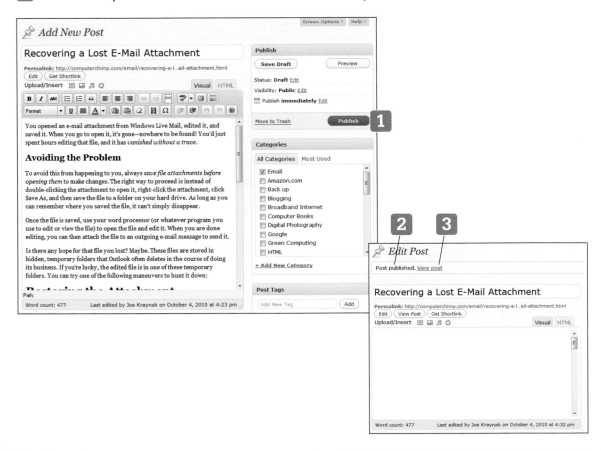

HOT TIP: Schedule publication. In the Publish menu, next to the Publish immediately option, click Edit, choose the desired date and time, then click the Publish button.

DID YOU KNOW?
You can make posts or pages private or require visitors to enter a password to view them. Prior to publishing, click Edit, in the Publish box next to the Visibility Public option, then enter your preferences.

Edit a page or post

After publishing a page or post, you can edit it and even change its Publish settings to change its visibility or else unpublish previously published content.

1 Open the Posts menu and click Posts or open the Pages menu and click Pages.

2 Below the page or post you want to edit, click the Edit link.

3 Edit the page or post.

4 Click Update.

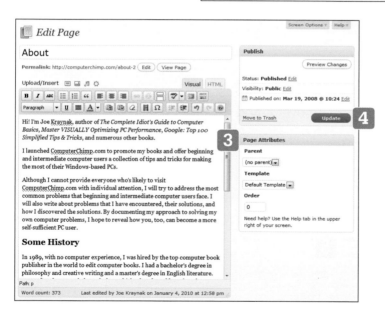

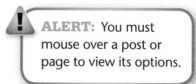

> ⚠ **ALERT:** You must mouse over a post or page to view its options.

🔥 **HOT TIP:** If more than one user manages the site, you can select a different user as the author for a page or post. When adding or editing a page or post, scroll down to the Author box and choose the desired user.

❓ **DID YOU KNOW?**
The Quick Edit option only enables you to change settings for the post or page, including its title, author, categories and whether or not to allow comments or pings.

Delete a page or post

You can delete a page or post at any time, as shown below.

1 Open the Posts menu and click Posts or open the Pages menu and click Pages.

2 Mouse over the page or post you want to delete and click Trash.

3 Click Trash to view deleted items.

4 To restore an item, mouse over it and click Restore.

5 To permanently delete an item, mouse over it and click Delete Permanently.

? DID YOU KNOW?

Each Pages and Posts page displays only up to 20 pages or posts. You can see more by clicking the numbers above and below the lists.

HOT TIP: If you are having trouble finding a page or post, use the Search Posts or Search Pages box in the upper right-hand corner of the Pages or Posts page to search for an item by keywords in its title or body.

Back up your site's content

The most valuable part of your site is its contents, so back it up regularly. WordPress features a convenient backup option.

1 Open the Tools menu and click Export.

2 Click Download Export File.

3 Save the export file to a folder on your computer.

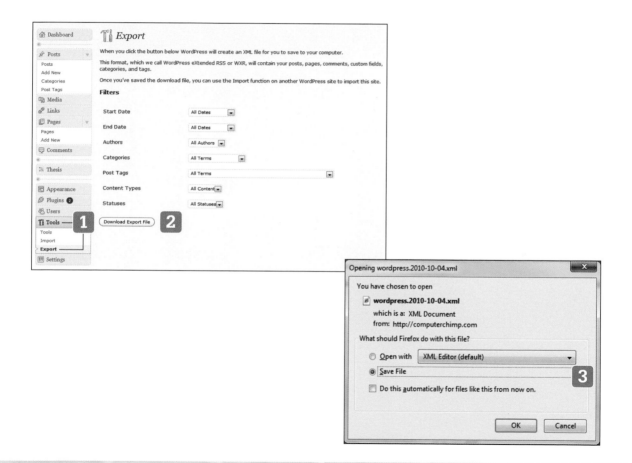

 **HOT TIP:** Exporting is also useful if you need to move your site.

HOT TIP: You can use the exported file to restore your site if it crashes. Just reinstall WordPress, as explained in Chapter 4, then use the Tools, Import option.

11 Configure a template with cascading style sheets (CSS)

Introduction

Every WordPress template has one or more cascading style sheets (CSS), each of which contains a collection of style rules that apply formatting to various HTML elements, including headings, paragraphs, lists and images. To change the appearance of any element on your site, you must edit the style that controls it. You can also create your own styles by specifying the element you want to format along with the formatting you want to apply to it.

This chapter shows you how to open a theme's style sheet file (typically named 'style.css') and edit style rules to change the appearance and/or position of elements on your Web pages and blog.

The steps given in this chapter assume that you are logged in to WordPress. See Chapter 4 for details on logging in.

Open a style sheet to edit

Before you can edit styles in a theme's style sheet, you must open it in WordPress. In most cases, you will be editing a file named 'styles.css', which contains most of the style rules for the template.

1 Open the Appearance menu and click Editor.

2 Under Styles, click the style file you want to edit.

3 Create or edit styles.

4 Click Update File to save your changes.

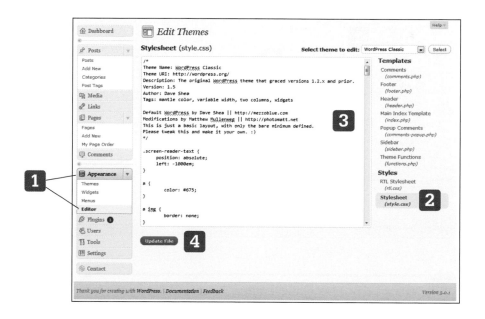

HOT TIP: You can edit any installed theme. Open the Select theme to edit menu (upper right-hand corner), choose the theme to edit, then click Select.

ALERT: Select all of the style rules in the style sheet you are about to edit, copy them and paste them in a plain text file, so that you have a backup copy, in case you make a mistake when editing the style sheet.

Edit a style rule

When working with an existing theme, you may not need to create your own style rules. The existing style sheet should contain rules for all HTML elements. To change the appearance or position of an element, just edit its style rule.

1 Identify the selector that targets the element you want to format.

2 Edit the style declarations that control the element's appearance.

3 Click Update File to save the changes.

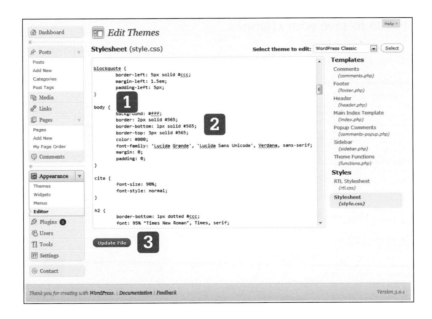

> **SEE ALSO:** One of the biggest challenges is identifying the style rule that controls an element's appearance! For help, use Firebug, as explained at the end of this chapter.

WHAT DOES THIS MEAN?

Selector: the part of a style rule that targets an element for formatting.

Style declaration: the part of a style rule that applies formatting to the element. Each style declaration is a 'property:value;' pair.

Property: a characteristic of an element to be formatted, such as its colour.

Value: the specific formatting to apply, such as blue.

Define class selector style rules

You can create class selectors with any name you like – such as 'alignleft' or 'no-bullets' – and use them to apply styles to HTML elements depending on how the elements are used. For example, you can use three different classes to align images left, right or centre them.

1 Create a class selector style rule, naming the selector whatever you like (with no spaces).

2 Click Update File.

3 Add a class attribute to the HTML element you want to format with a value that matches the class selector.

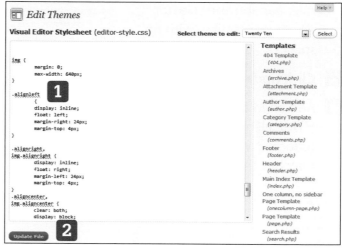

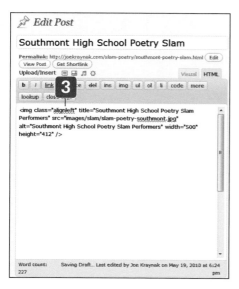

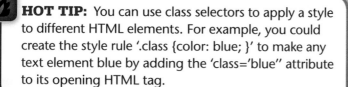

? DID YOU KNOW?
Class selectors always start with a full stop.

HOT TIP: You can use class selectors to apply a style to different HTML elements. For example, you could create the style rule '.class {color: blue; }' to make any text element blue by adding the 'class='blue'' attribute to its opening HTML tag.

Define ID selector style rules

An ID selector enables you to apply a specific style to one instance of an HTML element on a page. Because of this, ID selectors are commonly used to apply styles to headers and footers, which appear only once on a page.

1 Create an ID selector, style rule, naming the selector whatever you like (with no spaces).

2 Click Update File.

3 Add an id attribute to the HTML element you want to format with a value that matches the class selector.

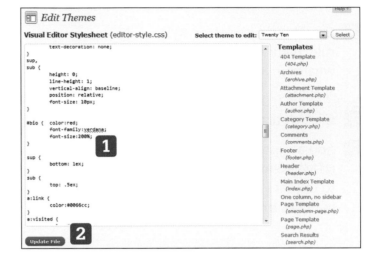

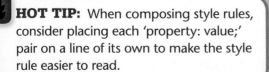

? **DID YOU KNOW?**

ID selectors always start with a hash mark – '#'

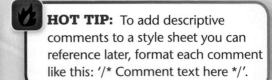

🔥 **HOT TIP:** When composing style rules, consider placing each 'property: value;' pair on a line of its own to make the style rule easier to read.

🔥 **HOT TIP:** To add descriptive comments to a style sheet you can reference later, format each comment like this: '/* Comment text here */'.

Apply style properties with <div> and <span> tags

You can use HTML <div> and <span> tags in tandem with class and ID selectors to create your own HTML elements and format them with style rules.

1 Bracket any text you want to format with an opening and closing <div> or <span> tag.

2 Add a class or ID attribute to the opening <div> or <span> tag.

3 Create a style rule using a class or ID selector that matches the attribute.

1 **2**

```
<div class="bio">

<h2>Biography</h2>

<img class="alignleft" title="Joe Kraynak" src="http://joekraynak.com
/images/joekraynak.jpg" alt="Joe Kraynak" width="154" height="155"
/><strong>Joe Kraynak</strong> is a freelance writer/editor who has
authored and co-authored numerous books, including <em>Flipping
Houses For Dummies</em>, <em>Bipolar Disorder For Dummies</em>,
<em>The Complete Idiot's Guide to Computer Basics</em>, <em>Take
the Mic</em>, <em>Stage a Poetry Slam</em>, and <em>Master
Visually: Creating Web Pages</em>.

</div>    1
```

```
.bio {                         3
        color: white;
        font-size: 13px;
        background: black;
{
```

HOT TIP: Use <div> tags to bracket one or more HTML elements. Use <span> tags to apply formatting within an HTML element, such as a few words within a sentence.

HOT TIP: You can apply an inline style by adding a style attribute to the element's opening tag, like this: '<p style = "font-size:10px;">'. Do this sparingly, though, as, otherwise, it defeats the purpose of keeping the HTML and CSS separate.

Assign CSS measurement values

Whenever you need to specify the size of any element, you need to specify a unit of measure, such as px (pixels), % (percentage), em (em unit), ex (ex unit), cm (centimetres), mm (millimetres), pt (points) and pc (picas) .

1 Specify height, width, font size, border width, image dimensions and so on with CSS measurement values.

2 Use px for precise measurements.

3 Use % or em units to enable elements to scale dynamically to browser settings.

```
h6 {
        font-size: 0.9em;          1
}

table {
        border: 1px solid #e7e7e7 !important;
        text-align: left;              2
        margin: 0 -1px 24px 0;              3
        width: 100%;
        border-collapse: collapse;
        border-spacing: 0;
}
tr th,
thead th {
        border: none !important;
        color: #888;
        font-size: 12px;
        font-weight: bold;
        line-height: 18px;
        padding: 9px 24px;
}
```

? DID YOU KNOW?

Most measurements in CSS are in pixels, percentages or em units:

- **Pixel** a single dot on a computer screen
- **em** a unit equivalent to the current font size, so 1.5ems is 150 per cent of the current font size
- **ex** a unit equivalent to the current font height, which is about half the font size
- **point** approximately .35 mm
- **pica** 12 points.

Define font properties

To control the appearance of text, define an element's font properties, including font family, size, style, variant and weight.

1 Identify the selector for the text element you want to format.

2 Add the font declaration in the format '{font: style variant weight size/line height family; }'.

3 Alternatively, add individual font declarations using the properties font-style, font-variant, font-weight, font-size/line-height, font-family.

```
blockquote {font: italic small-caps bold 11px/13px georgia; }
```

```
blockquote {
        font-style: italic;
        font-variant: small-caps;
        font-weight: bold;
        font-size: 11px;
        line-height: 13px;
        font-family: georgia;
}
```

HOT TIP: To specify a font family for the entire page, define the font properties using the body selector.

DID YOU KNOW?
Common font options include 'font-style: italic;','font-variant: small-caps;' and 'font-weight: bold;'.

DID YOU KNOW?
Common font families include the following:

Arial	**Arial Black**	Comic Sans MS	Courier New
Georgia	Lucida Console	Tahoma	Times New Roman

Define text properties

Text properties enable you to control other characteristics of the text, including its colour, indents and alignment.

1 Identify the selector for the text element you want to format.

2 Add the desired text style declarations.

1

```
.center {
        text-align: center;
        vertical-align: middle;
        color: blue;
}
```
2

Style declarations include the following:

Property	Value
color	colour name or code
text-align	left, right, centre or justify
text-decoration	underline or strikethrough (called 'line-through' in CSS)
text-indent	indent first line by a specified amount
vertical-align	baseline, sub, super, top, middle, bottom.

Assign CSS colour values

CSS style rules enable you to apply colour to various HTML elements, including paragraphs, headings, borders and backgrounds.

1 Use the color property to apply colour to text elements.

2 Use the border-color property to apply colour to borders.

3 Use the background-color property to apply colour to backgrounds.

```
p, h1, h2, h3 {
        color: white;
}
```
1

```
blockquote {
        border-width: 4px;
        border-style: groove;
        border-color: blue;
}
```
2

```
.sidebar {
        background: #F0F8FF;
}
```
3

 HOT TIP: You can use the background property instead of background colour – '{background: white}', for example.

 HOT TIP: You can use the border property to apply multiple border styles, including colour – '{border: 2px dotted blue; }', for example.

 SEE ALSO: You can specify some colours by name, but, typically, hex values are used. See Chapter 5 for more on colour.

Format unordered lists

You can change the appearance of the bullets used for unordered lists or remove the bullets entirely.

1 Identify the selector for unordered lists.

2 Specify the type of bullet you want to use with the list-style-type property.

3 Alternatively, specify a small image to use as the bullet.

1

2
```
ul {
        list-style-type: square;
        margin: 0 0 18px 1.5em;
}
```

3
```
ul {
        list-style-image: url('images/bullet.gif');
}
```

? DID YOU KNOW?

Unordered list style types include the following:

- **none**   no bullet
- **disc**   filled-in circle – this is the default setting
- **circle**   outline of a circle
- **square**   filled-in square.

WHAT DOES THIS MEAN?

Unordered list: a list without numbers.

 SEE ALSO: If you use an image as the bullet, be sure to upload the image first. See Chapter 3 for details on uploading files.

Format ordered lists

Ordered lists are numbered lists. By default, Arabic numerals appear next to list items. You can use different numerals instead, though, including Roman numerals.

1 Identify the selector for ordered lists.

2 Specify the type of numeral to use with the 'list-style-type' property.

1

```
ol {
        list-style-type: decimal; 2
        margin: 0 0 18px 1.5em;
}

ol ol {
        list-style-type: upper-alpha;
}

ol ol ol {
        list-style-type: lower-roman;
}

ol ol ol ol {
        list-style-type: lower-alpha;
}
```

▶ **SEE ALSO:** You can also format ordered and unordered lists by changing the space between items in the lists. See Set margins and add padding around elements a bit later in this chapter.

? **DID YOU KNOW?**

Ordered list style types include the following, which are excellent for formatting list items in an outline:

• **upper-roman**   I, II, III, IV and so on

• **upper-alpha**   A, B, C, D, E and so on

• **lower-roman**   i, ii, iii, iv, v and so on

• **lower-alpha**   a, b, c, d, e and so on.

Define hyperlink properties

Hyperlinks typically change their appearance depending on their state – that is, when unvisited, visited, with the mouse pointer over the link and so on. You can control how they appear in different states by using selectors to target pseudo elements.

1 Identify the pseudo element for the desired hyperlink state.

2 Edit the style declaration to specify the appearance of the link in that state.

3 The hyperlink's appearance then changes based on its state.

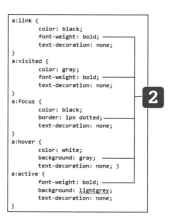

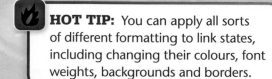

HOT TIP: You can apply all sorts of different formatting to link states, including changing their colours, font weights, backgrounds and borders.

Create a box

To control the position of elements on a page, CSS uses the box model. With the box model, you may treat every element as though it is inside a box.

1 In your HTML document, enclose all the elements you want to include in the box between <div> tags.

2 To the opening <div> tag, add a unique class or ID attribute.

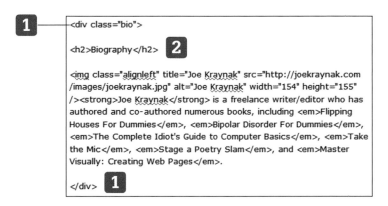

3 Create a class or ID style that specifies the box's height and width.

4 Float the box left or right.

Add borders

The CSS box model enables you to add borders around any HTML element.

1 Add the border property to an element's style rule.

2 Specify the border's width, style and colour.

```
.bio {
        height: 200px;
        width: 150px;
        float: right;
   1 —border: 4px ridge blue;        2
}
```

? DID YOU KNOW?

You can set a border's width and style separately for each side of the box – '{border-style-top: solid; border-style-left: dotted; border-width-bottom: 2px; border-width-right: 3px;}', for example.

 HOT TIP: Border styles include dotted, dashed, solid, double, groove, ridge, inset and outset patterns.

Set margins and add padding around elements

To create space between elements, specify the margin and padding settings.

1 Specify how much padding you want inserted to create space between the element and its border.

2 Specify the margins, to create space outside the border.

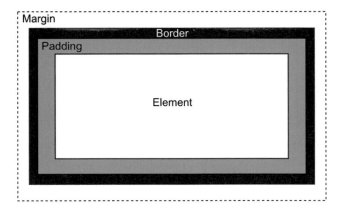

```
.bio {
        height: 200px;
        width: 150px;
        float: right;
        border: 4px ridge blue;
        padding: 5px;
        margin: 10px;
}
```

ALERT: The actual width and height of an element includes its width and height plus margins, padding and border widths.

WHAT DOES THIS MEAN?

Margin: the space around an element outside its border that is transparent.

Padding: the space between an element and its border – it may have a background colour or image.

Add a background image

You can apply background properties to HTML elements or divisions to add colour, shading or even a background image.

1 Add the '{background-image:url('wp-content/images/img.jpg');}' style declaration to the element.

2 Specify the background image's position.

3 Specify whether or not you want the image to repeat.

```
body {
        background-image:url('wp-content/images/background.jpg'); 1
        background-position: center center; 2
        background-repeat: no-repeat; 3
}
```

 SEE ALSO: Background images are commonly used in headers. See Chapter 7 for details.

ALERT: The steps given here assume you have uploaded the image you want to use. See Chapter 3 for details on how to do so.

 HOT TIP: Use the body selector to have a background image appear behind the entire body of a page.

WHAT DOES THIS MEAN?

Background image: an image that appears behind the element, typically behind the text.

Position elements on a page

You can position elements anywhere on a page by using the CSS position property. It is especially useful for positioning box elements on a page. If elements overlap, use z-index to control which one appears on top. So, an element with a z-index 1 value would be on top of one with a z-index 0 value, for example.

1 Identify the element's selector.

2 Specify a positioning method.

3 Specify the position.

1

```
.bio {
        height: 200px;
        width: 150px;
        float: right;
        border: 4px ridge blue;
        padding: 5px;
        margin: 10px;
        position: relative;    2
        left: 20px;
        top: 10px;    3
}
```

WHAT DOES THIS MEAN?

Positioning method: a CSS property that specifies how positioning specifications are applied. The CSS has four positioning properties:

- **static** the default setting, elements are positioned according to the normal flow of the page

- **fixed** position is relative to the browser window and does not move even if a window's contents are scrolled

- **relative** position is relative to its normal position according to the normal flow of the page

- **absolute** position is relative to the first parent element that has a position other than static; otherwise, position is relative to the top left-hand corner of the page.

Add a scroll bar

If a box contains more content than fits inside the box, some of it will spill over its borders. You can use the overflow property to add a scroll bar to the box to prevent this from occurring.

1 Identify the selector for the box.

2 Add the 'overflow: auto;' declaration to the style.

```
.scroll {
        margin-bottom: 10px;
        height: 350px;
        width: 400px;
        padding-left: 10px;
        overflow: auto;
        position: relative;  left: 10%;
        box-shadow: 5px 5px 5px #666;
}
```

HOT TIP: Scrolling is an excellent choice if you have a long list that you want to display in a small amount of space. You can add an inline style to the lists opening tag – '<ul style="overflow:scroll">', for example.

DID YOU KNOW?

Other overflow properties include the following:

* **hidden** overflow content is not shown
* **scroll** displays a scroll bar regardless of whether the content fits.

Download and install Firebug

Identifying which selector controls the appearance of an element can be quite a challenge. Fortunately, Firebug, an add-on for the Mozilla Firefox Web browser can help. Here's how to download and install it, then, next, it'll show you how to use it.

1 In Mozilla Firefox, click Tools, then Add-ons.

2 Click Get Add-ons.

3 Search for Firebug.

4 Click Add to Firefox.

5 Click Firebug.

6 Click Install Now.

7 When prompted, restart Firefox.

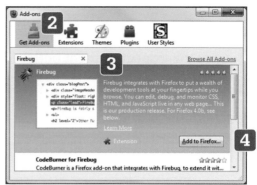

 ALERT: This task assumes Mozilla Firefox has been installed. If you do not have the Firefox Web browser, download and install it at www.mozilla.com.

 DID YOU KNOW?
Firebug displays the HTML and CSS for selected elements, so you can see what is going on behind the scenes.

 SEE ALSO: Chapter 5 covers another valuable Firefox add-on called ColorZilla, which enables you to inspect colours.

Use Firebug to inspect an element's CSS

To view the HTML tags and CSS styles that control the position and appearance of an element, use Firebug to inspect it.

1 Open the Web page that contains the element you want to inspect.

2 Click the Firebug icon.

3 Click the Inspect Element button.

4 Click the element you want to inspect.

5 Check the element's HTML.

6 Identify the element's selector and style declarations.

HOT TIP: If that big grey box in the upper left-hand corner gets in the way, you can drag it out of the way.

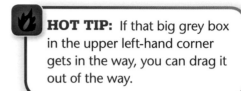

HOT TIP: Click the Layout tab, just above the CSS style pane, to view a graphic of the object's padding, border and margin.

HOT TIP: Use Firebug to troubleshoot problems with HTML and CSS when an element is not appearing as you expect.

12 Configure your site's design with a premium theme

Introduction

Premium and some higher-end free themes feature their own control panel(s) for customising sites without having to edit style rules. To change a font's style, for example, you simply select the font you want to use for an element from a list. To change the font's size, you simply type the size you want to use. This makes the most common adjustments very easy to do.

Making less common adjustments, however, can actually be more involved than simply editing a CSS file. You may need to shift your thinking to adapt to a different system of customisation. This chapter cannot possibly cover all of the variations you may encounter among custom themes, but it does provide the guidance you need to deal with the unexpected.

This chapter uses the Thesis Theme as its example, which you can obtain at http://diythemes.com.

Adjust the theme's design options

A theme's design options are what you modify to change the appearance and layout of pages and the appearance of elements on pages.

1 Open the theme's menu and click Design Options.

2 Click a plus sign to expand an option box.

3 Enter your preferences.

4 Save your changes.

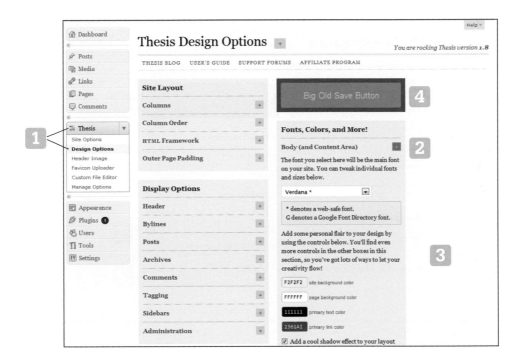

? DID YOU KNOW?

Design options may enable you to change the number, width and arrangement of columns; font family, size and colour for text elements; background colours; padding and margins for boxed elements and more.

▶ SEE ALSO: Use the Firebug plugin to identify the options that control the appearance of individual elements, as explained in Chapter 11.

Adjust the theme's site options

Site options focus more on a site's content than on its appearance. For example, you can adjust site options to control which pages appear in a navigation bar or add a tracking script to your site so that you can monitor traffic.

 Open the theme's menu and click Site Options.

 Click a plus sign to expand an option box.

 Enter your preferences.

 Save your changes.

> **SEE ALSO:** For more on adding a tracking script to your site, see Chapter 16.

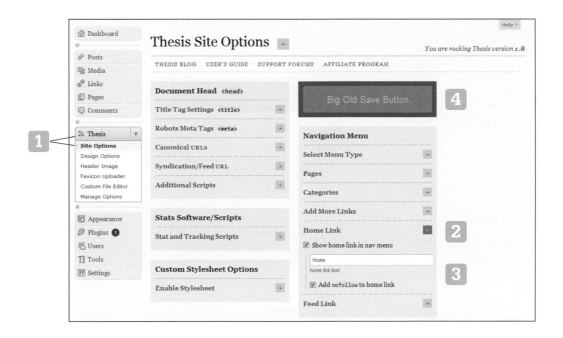

HOT TIP: Check site options for home page SEO options, which enable you to enter additional information about your home page that may help search engines properly index your site.

HOT TIP: Check if your theme has links to a user's guide or support forums for additional information and guidance.

Adjust column numbers and widths

Most premium themes enable you to easily control the number of columns (1, 2 or 3) and their relative widths.

1 Click Design Options in the theme's menu and expand the Columns option.

2 Choose the desired number of columns.

3 Specify each column's width.

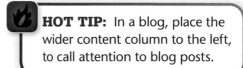

HOT TIP: In a blog, place the wider content column to the left, to call attention to blog posts.

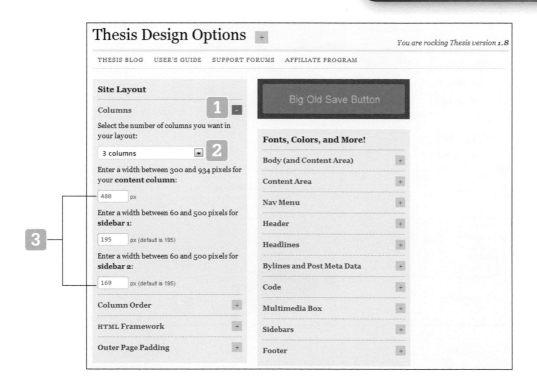

Thesis Design Options +

You are rocking Thesis version 1.8

THESIS BLOG   USER'S GUIDE   SUPPORT FORUMS   AFFILIATE PROGRAM

Site Layout

Columns **1** −

Select the number of columns you want in your layout:

3 columns ▾ **2**

Enter a width between 300 and 934 pixels for your **content column:**

480 px

Enter a width between 60 and 500 pixels for **sidebar 1:**

3

195 px (default is 195)

Enter a width between 60 and 500 pixels for **sidebar 2:**

169 px (default is 195)

Column Order +

HTML Framework +

Outer Page Padding +

Big Old Save Button

Fonts, Colors, and More!

Body (and Content Area) +

Content Area +

Nav Menu +

Header +

Headlines +

Bylines and Post Meta Data +

Code +

Multimedia Box +

Sidebars +

Footer +

? DID YOU KNOW?

To preview your changes, right-click the site's title in the upper left-hand corner of the WordPress screen and click Open in New Tab.

! ALERT: When specifying column widths, be careful to ensure that, when added together, they do not exceed the total width of the page.

Change background colours

Themes typically have two background settings: site background, for the space around the page, and page background, for the page itself.

1 In Design Options, expand the Body (and Content Area) option.

2 Click the box for the colour you want to change.

3 Use the controls that appear to specify the desired colour.

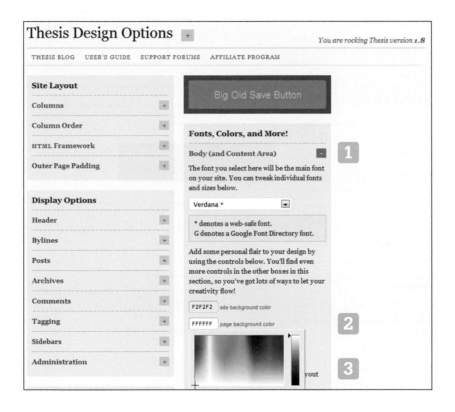

 DID YOU KNOW?
The Body (and Content Area) option may contain additional choices for adding special effects, such as shadows.

 SEE ALSO: For more on adding colours to a site and creating an attractive colour scheme, see Chapter 5.

Change a font's family, size and colour

Premium themes shine when it comes to formatting text. You can instantly change a font's family, size and colour for a variety of elements, including headings, body text and bylines.

1 In Design Options, expand the options for the text you want to format.

2 Choose the desired font family.

3 Choose the size you want.

4 Choose the desired text colour.

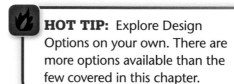

HOT TIP: Explore Design Options on your own. There are more options available than the few covered in this chapter.

WHAT DOES THIS MEAN?

Web-safe: font families and colours that most Web browsers display properly. Fonts include Arial, Arial Black, Courier New, Georgia, Times New Roman and Verdana.

Use themes within a premium theme

Some themes include additional themes that you can use for individual pages or posts. Thesis, for example, includes a no sidebars theme.

1 Create a new page as you normally would.

2 Open the Template list.

3 Click the template you want to use for the page.

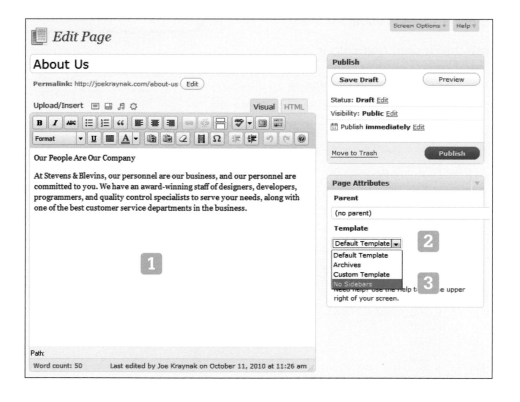

SEE ALSO: For more on creating pages and posts, see Chapter 10.

Override design elements with custom CSS

Although themes make customising some elements easy, the options available via the theme's control panels may not cover everything you want to do. In such cases, you may need to create your own custom styles.

1 Use Firebug to identify the element you want to format.

2 Click Custom File Editor.

3 Choose the custom.css file, if necessary, and click Edit selected file.

4 Create a custom style to override the existing style or add to it.

5 Save your changes.

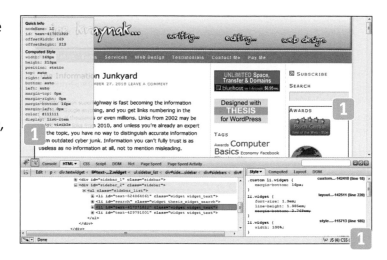

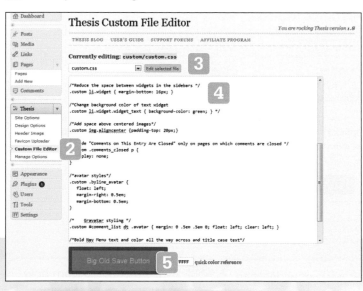

DID YOU KNOW?

The custom.css file enables you to keep all style changes in a single file without modifying the theme's core style sheet.

ALERT: Thesis has a 'custom. css' file that you can edit to add or modify styles. This may not be the case in all premium themes.

SEE ALSO: For more on CSS style rules, see Chapter 11.

Add a header image

Most premium themes enable you to add your own header image via the theme's control panel. The steps below show you how to add a header image in Thesis.

1 From the theme's menu, select Header Image.

2 Click Browse.

3 Click the header image you want to use.

4 Click Open.

5 Click Upload.

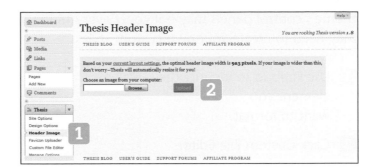

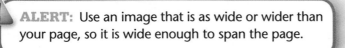

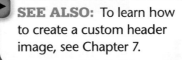

ALERT: Use an image that is as wide or wider than your page, so it is wide enough to span the page.

SEE ALSO: To learn how to create a custom header image, see Chapter 7.

Add pages to the Navigation menu

The Navigation menu displays the names of pages and visitors can click them to view each one. You can choose which pages you want to appear in the menu.

1 From the theme's menu, click Site Options.

2 Expand the Pages menu.

3 Select each page you want to appear on the menu.

4 Drag and drop pages to change their order.

5 Edit the page name, if necessary, to shorten it.

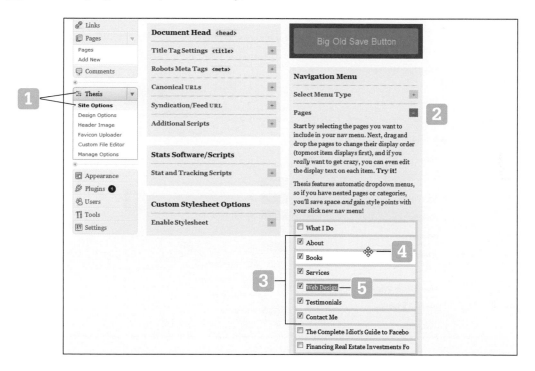

HOT TIP: WordPress has its own Navigation Bar feature, so you should be able to add a custom navigation bar to your site even if you don't have a premium theme.

Configure the Navigation menu

Most premium themes have a navigation bar that runs along the top, either above or below the header image. You should be able to change the appearance of the menu via the theme's control panel.

1 From the Thesis menu, select Design Options.

2 Expand Nav Menu.

3 Enter your preferences.

4 Save your changes.

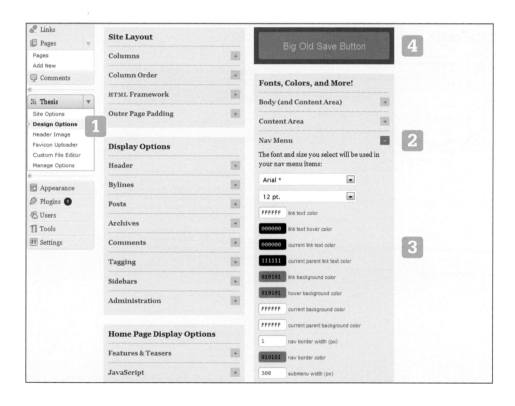

? **DID YOU KNOW?**

The Navigation menu's options enable you to change the font family, size and colour; the link text and background colour; and the border width and colour for the Navigation menu bar.

▶ **SEE ALSO:** To move the Navigation menu to after the header, see the next section.

Customise a theme with hooks

Thesis and other premium themes may enable you to use hooks to modify the position of elements on pages and perform other high-level customisation. The steps given below demonstrate how to use hooks in Thesis to move the Navigation menu from before to after the header.

1. From the theme's menu, select Custom File Editor.

2. Choose the custom_functions.php file and click Edit selected file.

3. Use 'remove_action' and 'add_action' to change the location of the hook.

4. Save your changes.

ALERT: Thesis has a 'custom_functions.php' file that you can edit to modify hook usage. This may not be the case in all premium themes.

DID YOU KNOW?
Hooks are so called because they enable developers to 'hook' plugins onto the WordPress platform to enhance it.

WHAT DOES THIS MEAN?
Hook: a script that enables developers to call functions at specific times to activate a plugin.

SEE ALSO: For more about hooks, visit http://codex.wordpress.org/Plugin_API.

13 Add graphics and videos to pages and posts

Introduction

Nothing livens up a website like images and video, but that means uploading images and video to the Web, then knowing how to insert and manipulate these media in your pages and posts. It is not very difficult, but the steps are somewhat involved, so let this chapter be your guide. Discover how to prepare images for insertion on Web pages, upload images and video and manage them online, control the way text wraps around images and perform other tasks to make your images look their very best.

Establish a media management strategy

Before you can use images on your site, they must be stored somewhere online. You have several options.

1 One option is to upload the images to a folder in the 'public_html' folder.

2 Another is to upload images to a file-sharing site, such as Flickr.

3 Yet another option is to store the images in the WordPress Media Library.

ALERT: The options given here pertain only to images. See Upload a video to the Web near the end of this chapter for details on managing video online.

? DID YOU KNOW?
I prefer storing images in a separate images folder on my own hosting account for greater control, but storing them in the Media Library makes them more conveniently accessible.

SEE ALSO: For more on uploading files to your hosting account, see Chapter 3.

Adjust the quality and size of images

Prior to uploading images, adjust their quality and size using photo editing software. Here I show you how to prepare a photo in Picasa.

1 Open the photo in Picasa.

2 Click I'm Feeling Lucky.

3 Click Export.

4 Choose a folder to export to.

5 Specify image size and quality

6 Click Export.

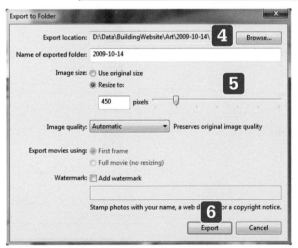

Upload images to the WordPress Media Library

If your media management strategy is to store images in the WordPress Media Library, follow the steps below to upload image files to it.

1 In WordPress, open the Media menu and click Add New.

2 Click Select Files.

3 Choose the files you want to upload and click Open.

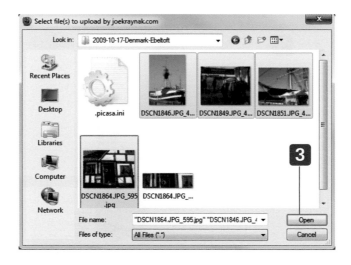

 HOT TIP: If you have a free Google account, you can upload images from Picasa to Google photo albums and then insert them into posts using their URLs.

 DID YOU KNOW?
As soon as you choose to open the image files, WordPress begins the upload.

Insert an image from the Media Library

If you store images in the WordPress Media Library, you are ready to insert them from the Media Gallery into pages and posts.

1 Position the insertion point so that it is where you want to place the image.

2 Click the Add an Image icon.

3 Click the Media Library tab.

4 Click Show next to the image you want to insert.

5 Enter your preferences.

6 Click Insert into Post or Insert into Page.

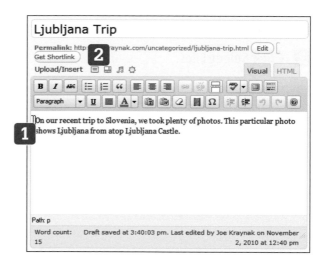

SEE ALSO: For details on how to create a page or post in WordPress, see Chapter 10. To learn more about the options in the Add an Image dialogue box, see the sections later in this chapter.

Insert an image using its URL

If an image is stored online but not in the WordPress Media Library, you insert it by specifying its URL – its web address.

1 Position the insertion point so that it is where you want to place the image.

2 Click the Add an Image icon.

3 Click the From URL tab.

4 Type or paste the image's URL in the Image URL box.

5 Type a title in the Image Title box.

6 Enter additional preferences.

7 Click Insert into Post or Insert into Page.

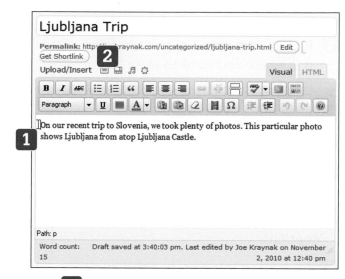

 HOT TIP: If you store your images somewhere else, open the image in a Web browser, then copy its URL from the browser's address bar.

Insert a thumbnail image

Thumbnail images are great for creating online photo galleries, because you can fit more images in the available space than when they are full size. Here's how to insert a thumbnail version of an image from the Media Library.

1 Position the insertion point so that it is where you want to place the image.

2 Click the Add an Image icon.

3 Click the Media Library tab.

4 Click Show next to the image you want to insert.

5 Select Thumbnail from the Size options.

6 Click Insert into Post or Insert into Page.

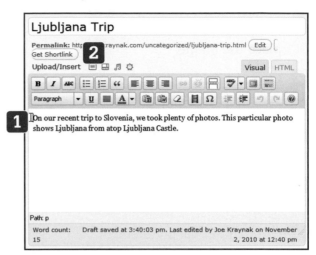

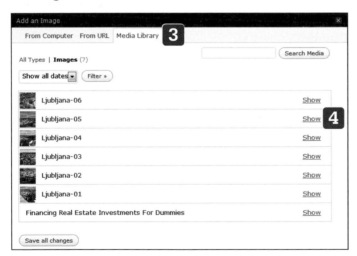

WHAT DOES THIS MEAN?

Thumbnail image: a smaller version of an image that links to the full-size image, so users have the option of viewing the larger version.

Resize an image

You can enter image dimensions when you insert the image, but resizing it after inserting is often best.

 Click the image to select it.

 Drag a corner handle to resize it.

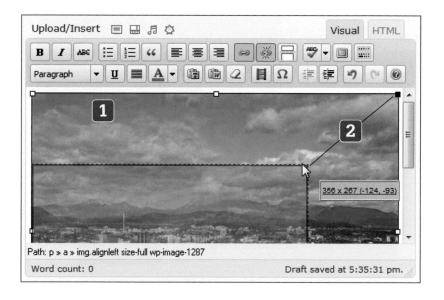

HOT TIP: If you click the image and the handles do not appear, try right-clicking the image, clicking a select option, then clicking the image again.

ALERT: Be sure to drag a *corner* handle, so that the dimensions of the image retains the same proportions – otherwise, the image will appear distorted.

Edit an image in WordPress

After inserting an image, you can change its properties by editing it. Here's how.

1 Click the image in the post or page.

2 Click the Edit Image button.

3 Enter your preferences.

4 Click Update.

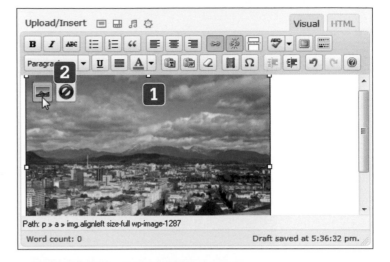

Align an image

When you insert or edit an image, you can specify an alignment preference: none, left, centre, or right. Find out how to change the alignment after inserting an image.

1 Click the image.

2 Click the Edit Image button.

3 Select your alignment preference.

4 Click Update.

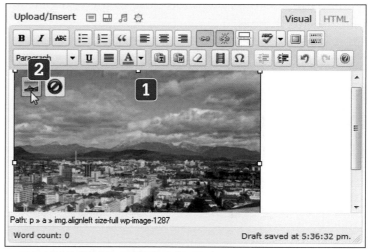

Add space between image and text

If an image's borders seem too close to the text that surrounds it, you can adjust how much space there is.

1 Click the image in the post or page.

2 Click the Edit Image button.

3 Click the Advanced Settings tab.

4 Enter the vertical and horizontal space values in pixels.

5 Click Update.

ALERT: Adjusting the space around an image (padding) is best done by editing the style that controls that space, as explained in Chapter 11. Use the Advanced Settings to adjust space only if one specific image is giving you problems rather than generally.

SEE ALSO: This action adds an inline style to the image that controls its margins. See Chapter 11 for more on inline styles.

Add a border to an image

If you think an image will look better with a border around it, you can add one when you insert or edit an image. Below are the steps you need to take to add a border after inserting an image.

1 Click the image.

2 Click the Edit Image button.

3 Click the Advanced Settings tab.

4 Type the desired border width in pixels.

5 Click Update.

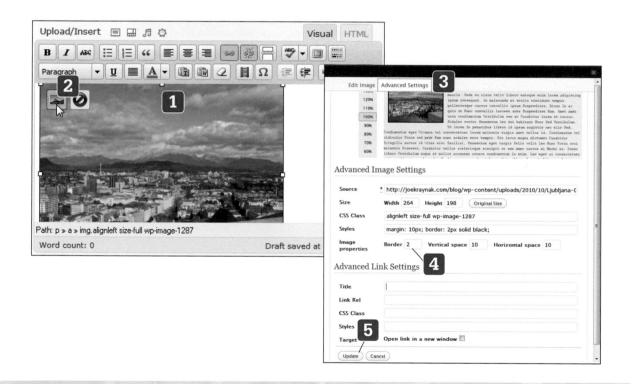

SEE ALSO: You can add borders to other HTML elements, too. See Chapter 11 for details.

HOT TIP: Your template's style sheet provides you with much more control over image borders than the steps given here. See Chapter 11 for details on editing styles in a style sheet.

Create an image link

An image can function as a link, so visitors can click the image to access another page or website.

1 Click the image in the post or page.

2 Click the Edit Image button.

3 Type the URL of the site or page you want the image to link to.

4 Click Update.

Specify alternative text

Some users may not be able to see your images or choose not to display them. In such cases, your site can display a description of the image.

1 Click the image in the post or page.

2 Click the Edit Image button.

3 Click in the Edit Alternate Text box and type a description of the image.

4 Click Update.

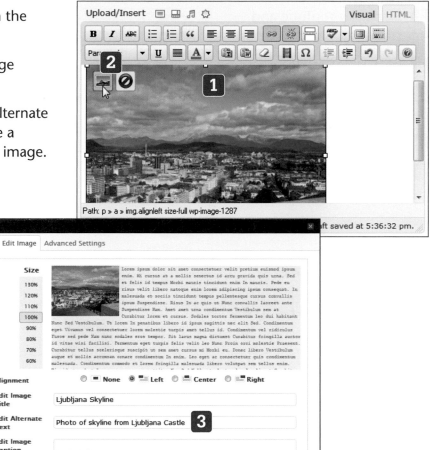

 DID YOU KNOW?

You should include an alternative text (alternate text in American programs) description for every image to assist the visually impaired as there are special Web browsers available to 'read' text to users.

Upload a video to the Web

One of the best and easiest ways to include video on your site is to upload the video to YouTube and then insert an embed code from the video into your page or post.

1 Sign in to YouTube and click the Upload link.

2 Click Upload video.

3 Choose a video file on your computer.

4 Click Open.

5 Copy the Embed code.

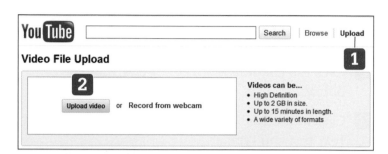

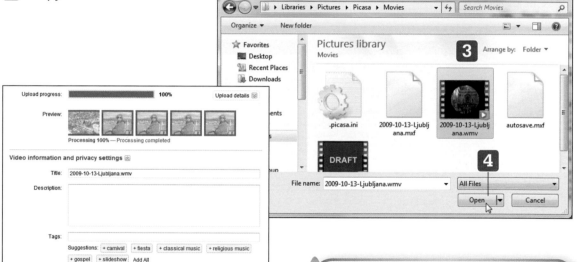

> ⚠ **ALERT:** You need a free YouTube account to do this. Go to www.youtube.com for details.

> 🔥 **HOT TIP:** YouTube is not the only video sharing site. Check out MetaCafe (www.metacafe.com), Google Videos (http://video.google.com) and Y! Video (http://video.yahoo.com).

Embed a video in a page or post

Once you've uploaded a video, the difficult job is done. Now, all you have to do is create a page or post and insert the embed code where you want the video to appear.

1 Create your page or post.

2 Change to HTML view by clicking the HTML tab.

3 Paste the embed code you copied in the previous section where you want the video to appear.

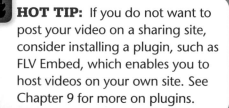 **HOT TIP:** If you do not want to post your video on a sharing site, consider installing a plugin, such as FLV Embed, which enables you to host videos on your own site. See Chapter 9 for more on plugins.

? DID YOU KNOW?
With the new HTML5 <video> element, soon you will be able to insert videos as easily as inserting images. As long as a video is in the proper format, browsers will be able to play the video without a plugin or YouTube.

14 Test and improve your site's speed

Introduction

Web users have little patience – they are not likely to wait more than a few seconds for a page to load, regardless of the content. If your page takes too long, they are likely to click the Back button and try a link to a different site.

In this chapter, you will discover two ways to test your site's speed and several techniques for fine-tuning your site so the pages load faster.

Test your Web page's loading speed at Pingdom.com

Several websites will test your Web page loading times for you and indicate which elements on each page take the longest times to load. The steps below show you how to test page loading speed at Pingdom.com.

1 Visit http://tools.pingdom.com.

2 Type or paste the address of a page on your site into the box.

3 Click Test Now.

4 Note the results.

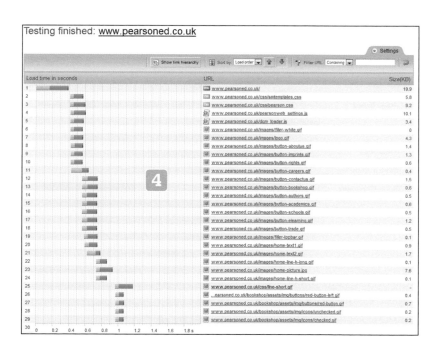

HOT TIP: Test more than once over a period of time as test results may be affected by factors other than those related to your site, such as traffic on the test site.

Download and install Google Page Speed

Google Page Speed is an add-on for the Mozilla Firefox Web browser. It tests Web page loading times, highlights problem areas and recommends modifications.

1 Use Firefox to go to http://code.google.com/speed/page-speed.

2 Click Install Page Speed.

3 Click the Install Page Speed button.

4 If prompted for confirmation, click Allow.

5 Click Install Now.

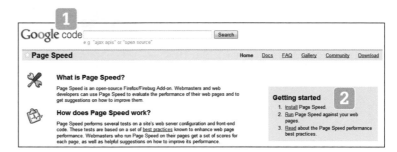

 **SEE ALSO:** Firebug must be installed prior to installing the Page Speed add-on. See Chapter 11 for instructions for installing Firebug.

ALERT: The steps here assume that you are using the Mozilla Firefox browser. You can install Firefox for free at www.mozilla.com/firefox.

Test page speed with Google Page Speed

Once you have installed Page Speed, you are ready to test a page. Here's what you do.

1 Open the page you want to test in Firefox.

2 Click the Firebug icon.

3 Click Page Speed.

4 Click Analyze Performance.

5 Click a plus sign next to an issue to view more details.

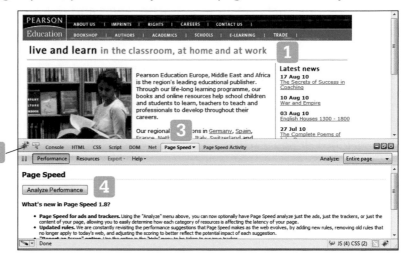

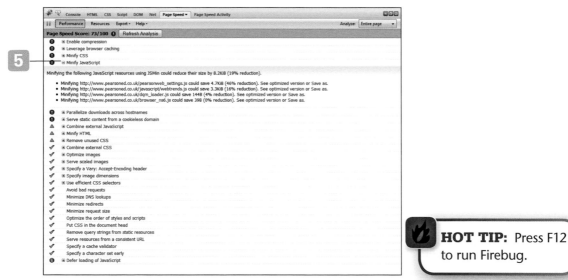

 HOT TIP: Press F12 to run Firebug.

 HOT TIP: Drag the top border of the Firebug bar to give Firebug more or less room to display results.

HOT TIP: Log in to WordPress on a separate tab. After fixing a problem, you can then flip back to the Page Analysis tab and click Refresh Analysis to check the results.

Speed up your site with W3 Total Cache

WordPress and other CMS's use a database to 'assemble' a page when users access it. A cache plugin, such as W3 Total Cache, saves and delivers a preassembled page, so it takes less time to load.

1 In WordPress, open the Plugins menu and click Add New.

2 Search for W3 Cache.

3 Under W3 Total Cache, click Install Now and click OK.

4 Click Activate Plugin.

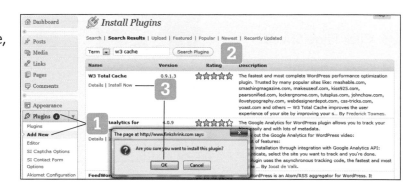

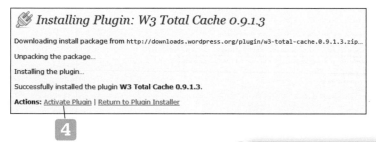

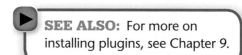

SEE ALSO: For more on installing plugins, see Chapter 9.

? DID YOU KNOW?

Before you will notice a difference, you must load a page so the cache plugin will cache it.

WHAT DOES THIS MEAN?

Cache: a performance feature that stores data temporarily in anticipation of delivering it on demand.

Adjust W3 Total Cache's settings

After installing W3 Total Cache, you may need to adjust its general settings to make sure that it is operating properly.

1 Open the Performance menu and click General Settings.

2 Place a tick in the Deselect this option to disable all caching functionality option box.

3 Open the Page Cache box and, by Page Cache Method, click Disk (enhanced).

4 Click Save changes.

5 Click Page Cache.

6 Make sure that all the options below General are selected, except for the last choice, which is optional.

7 Click Save changes.

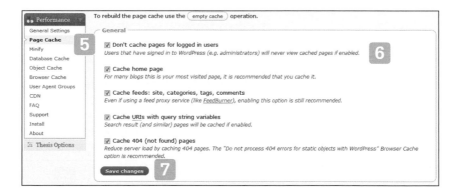

? DID YOU KNOW?

On the General Settings page, make sure that Minify, Database Cache, Object Cache and Browser Cache are all selected, too.

🔥 HOT TIP: Click FAQ on the Performance menu for additional information about W3 Total Cache.

Minify CSS and JavaScript files

After installing W3 Total Cache, you may need to adjust its general settings to make sure that it is operating properly.

1 Open the Performance menu and click Minify.

2 Click the Help button.

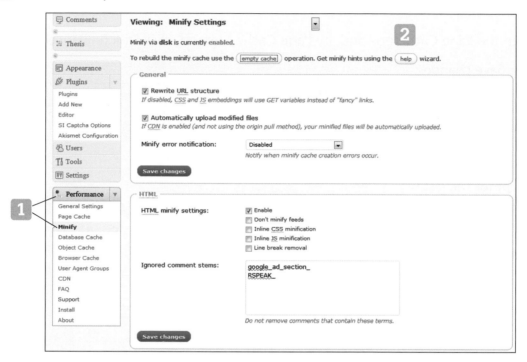

3 Under JavaScript, click Check/Uncheck All (this will put ticks in all the boxes or delete them).

4 Choose to embed each file after <body>.

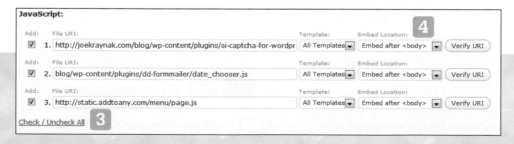

5 Under Cascading Style Sheets, below the list click Check/Uncheck All.

6 Click Apply & close.

7 Click Save changes.

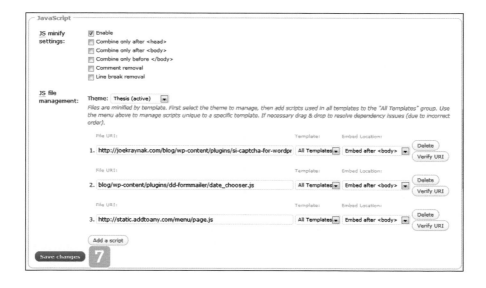

Reduce the size of an image file

Large, high-quality images can slow down your site considerably. Consider reducing the size and quality of images to improve the speed with which your pages load. See the steps below to learn how to export a smaller, lower-quality photo using Picasa.

1 Open a photo in Picasa.

2 Click Export.

3 Select a folder in which to store the exported file.

4 Reduce the size of the image using the slider.

5 Choose a lower-quality setting.

6 Click Export.

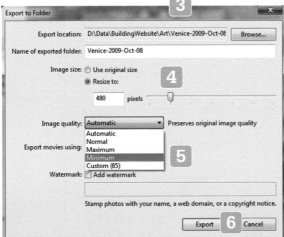

HOT TIP: You can download Picasa for free from http://picasa.google.com.

? DID YOU KNOW?
All graphics applications provide tools for resizing images and adjusting their quality.

► SEE ALSO: Chapter 13 shows you how to insert a thumbnail image that users can click to see the larger version.

15 Raise your site's search engine profile

Introduction

For people to be able to find your site, it needs to show up on the radar and, in this case, that is the search engines, including Google, Bing and Yahoo! Obviously, not every site can sit at the top of the search results for a specific keyword or phrase, but you can improve your ranking by employing a few savvy search engine optimisation (SEO) strategies and avoiding mistakes that can cause your site to be penalised.

This chapter reveals several SEO dos and don'ts that can raise your site's profile on the Web.

Register your site with search indexes

Search bots (Web spiders) should eventually find your pages and index them, but you can lend a helping hand by registering your site. Here's how to register your site with Google.

1 Visit www.google.co.uk/addurl.

2 Type your site's address in the URL box.

3 Type comments or keywords that describe the focus of your site.

4 Type the security word.

5 Click Add URL.

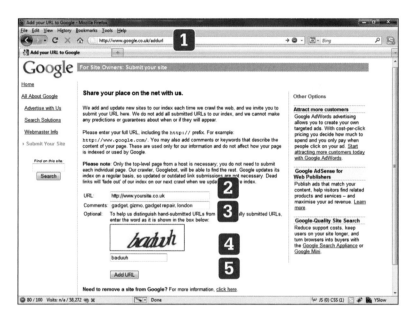

 ALERT: Search sites may take several weeks to index your site. Be patient as submitting your site repeatedly may result in your site being penalised.

 HOT TIP: Also register your site with Bing, Yahoo! and the Open Directory Project (dmoz.org).

WHAT DOES THIS MEAN?

Bot: short for 'robot', a bot is an automated utility.

Spider: a bot designed to search the Web for new or updated content to index.

SEO your content

One of the best ways to make sure search bots find your site and search engines properly index your site's content is to optimise the content in your pages and posts.

1 Add keywords to your page or post title.

2 Include keywords in the permalink.

3 Include keywords in the body of your page or post.

4 Give image and video files descriptive names.

5 Always include keyword optimised alternative text.

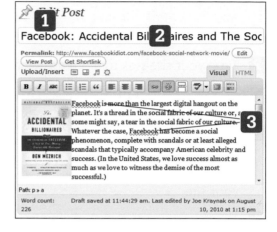

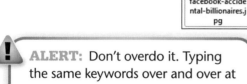

facebook-accide
ntal-billionaires.j
pg

ALERT: Don't overdo it. Typing the same keywords over and over at the end of a post or page may do more harm than good.

HOT TIP: Google gives more weight to larger images, so, if you use small images to make your pages load faster, link them to larger versions of the same image. See Chapter 13 for details.

WHAT DOES THIS MEAN?

Keyword: a term that captures the essence of content in a page or post and users are likely to use when searching for this content.

Implement an effective link strategy

Links to your site and within your site raise your site's profile and make it appear important. Also, if other sites are linking to yours, it must be important.

1. Add your site's address to all of your online profiles and accounts.

2. Post press releases that link to your site.

3. When you post comments on other sites, include your site address.

4. Add your business listing to online directories and include your site's address.

? DID YOU KNOW?

Internal links are also valuable. If you post something related to another post or page on your site, add a link to the related page or post.

 HOT TIP: If you belong to a professional organisation related to your site, you may be able to add your profile, complete with a link to your site. You can also, for business or professional sites, consider writing an article for an online publication in exchange for a link to your site. Another option is to promote your site through e-mail and by including its address on your business card and create a business or group page on Facebook with a link to your site.

Improve search engine optimisation with a sitemap plugin

Every site should have a sitemap that indicates the location of various pages and posts that comprise the site. Building and maintaining a site map is quite a chore, so install a plugin to do the work for you!

1 In WordPress, open the Plugins menu and click Add New.

2 Search for google xml.

3 Under Google XML Sitemaps, click Install Now.

4 Click OK to confirm.

5 Click Activate Plugin.

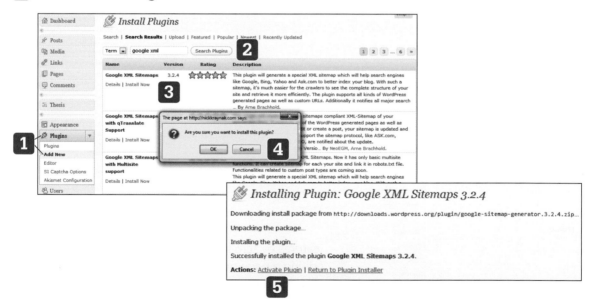

Improve search engine optimisation with an SEO plugin

Some templates include SEO optimisation features that enable you to add keywords and descriptions to pages and posts. If your theme does not have SEO features, install an SEO plugin.

1 In WordPress, open the Plugins menu and click Add New.

2 Search for SEO.

3 Under the SEO plugin you want, click Install Now.

4 Click OK to confirm.

5 Click Activate Plugin.

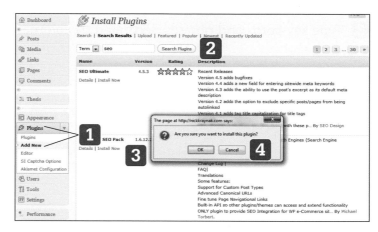

? DID YOU KNOW?
Several good WordPress SEO plugins are available, including All in One SEO Pack, HeadSpace2 and Platinum SEO.

Installing Plugin: All in One SEO Pack 1.6.12.2

Downloading install package from http://downloads.wordpress.org/plugin/all-in-one-seo-pack.zip...

Unpacking the package...

Installing the plugin... **5**

Successfully installed the plugin **All in One SEO Pack 1.6.12.2.**

Actions: Activate Plugin | Return to Plugin Installer

! ALERT: You can tell whether your theme has SEO features by scrolling down the screen for creating or editing a page or post and looking for boxes labelled SEO, Meta Keywords or Meta Description.

WHAT DOES THIS MEAN?

Meta: additional text that helps search engines find and index your site but is not shown to visitors.

Add SEO data to posts and pages

With an SEO-enabled theme or plugin, you can add data to posts and pages that is visible to search bots but not to users on your site.

1 Scroll down below the post and type a keyword-enhanced title.

2 Type a keyword-enhanced description.

3 Type keywords and phrases, separated by commas.

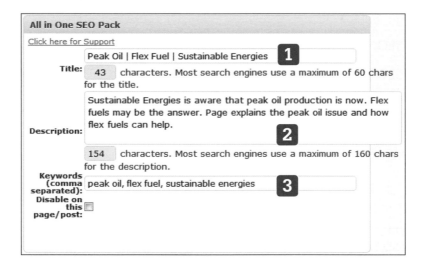

 HOT TIP: If your theme features its own control panel, check it for additional SEO options.

 ALERT: Steps may vary depending on which SEO features are installed, but the fields in which you type data should be similar to those shown here.

? DID YOU KNOW?
If you do not type an SEO title, WordPress uses the title of the page or post. An SEO title enables you to include additional keywords for the benefit of search engines. In either case, the title appears in the title bar of the user's browser.

Tag pages and posts

WordPress allows you to tag pages or posts with keywords, which search engines also use to determine relevance.

1 When creating or editing a post or page, type a keyword in the Post Tags box.

2 Click Add.

3 Click the 'X' next to a tag to remove it.

 DID YOU KNOW?
When creating categories for posts, include keywords wherever possible.

HOT TIP: You can add several tags at once by typing them in the Post Tags box and separating them with commas.

HOT TIP: Add the tag cloud widget to one of your sidebars to enable visitors to navigate the site by clicking tags. See Chapter 8 for more on widgets.

Install SEO Doctor for Firefox

SEO Doctor is an add-on for the Mozilla Firefox Web browser that performs a basic SEO audit of individual pages on your site, highlighting any potential problems.

1 In Mozilla Firefox, click Tools, Add-ons.

2 Click Get Add-ons.

3 Search for SEO.

4 Click SEO Doctor and click Add to Firefox.

5 Click Install Now.

6 When prompted, restart Firefox.

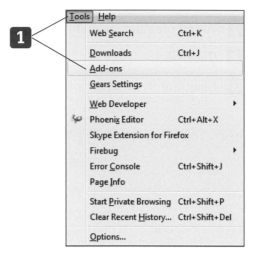

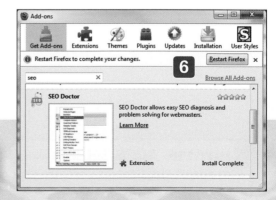

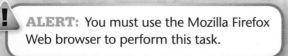

ALERT: You must use the Mozilla Firefox Web browser to perform this task.

Audit your site with SEO Doctor

SEO Doctor checks numerous factors that contribute to search engine optimisation, including your site's meta description, title tag and page rank flow, and offers guidance on how to improve it.

1 Open the page you want to audit in Firefox.

2 Click the page's SEO score.

3 Click an item to find out more about it.

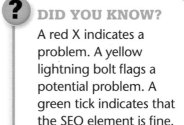

? DID YOU KNOW?
A red X indicates a problem. A yellow lightning bolt flags a potential problem. A green tick indicates that the SEO element is fine.

▶ SEE ALSO: SEO Doctor also checks for Web analytics, which you can learn more about in Chapter 16.

WHAT DOES THIS MEAN?
Page rank flow: the percentage of links pointing to resources on your site versus the total number of links.

16 Manage your site with Google Webmaster Tools and Analytics

Introduction

Google features a collection of Webmaster Tools that are essential for monitoring the performance of your site from an SEO standpoint, ensuring that your site has a functional sitemap, diagnosing crawl errors, identifying incoming links to your site and much more. In addition, Google Analytics can track user traffic on your site to provide valuable information on traffic volume and user behaviour. All of these tools are free and, now that you have a website, you should start taking advantage of them.

In this chapter, you will discover how to start exploring valuable data, statistics and diagnostic information about your site.

To perform the steps given in this chapter, you must have a Google account. Go to www.google.co.uk, click Sign In, click Create an Account Now, then follow the onscreen instructions to create your account.

Access Google's Webmaster Tools

You access Google's Webmaster Tools from your Google account settings. Sign in to your Google account and perform the following steps.

1 Visit www.google.co.uk/webmasters

2 Click Sign in to Webmaster Tools.

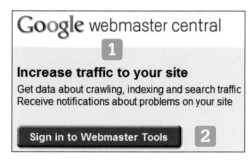

3 Sign in to your Google account.

 **DID YOU KNOW?**
Google Webmaster Tools provides insight into how Google and other search engines see your site.

 **DID YOU KNOW?**
Google Webmaster Tools shows keywords that users enter to find your site.

Add your site to Webmaster Tools

In order for Google Webmaster Tools to provide data about your site, you must add your site to it.

1. From the Webmaster Tools Home page, click Add a site.

2. Type the address of the site and click Continue.

3. Click Add a meta tag to your site's home page.

4. Copy the meta tag.

5. Paste the meta tag right after the opening <head> tag in Header (header.php) or into the header box in your theme's control panel and save your changes.

6. Return to Google Webmaster Tools and click Verify.

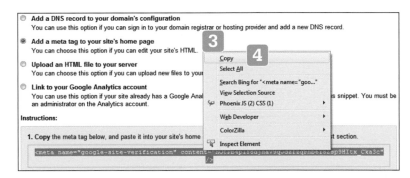

Header (header.php)   **Select theme**

```
<head>

<meta name="google-site-verification"
content="HOtPb4pIY8djhaV9qJdzfzqPhb6Y8Zsp9HItx_Cka3c" />

</head>
```

ALERT: The meta tag must appear between the opening and closing <head> tags near the top of the page. With some themes, you paste it in the Header (header.php) box. In other themes, you add it via the theme's control panel.

SEE ALSO: In Chapter 11, you edited a theme's Stylesheet (style.css) file. Opening and editing a theme's php file is very similar.

Check your site's configuration

Google Webmaster Tools provides important information about your site's configuration, including if it has a sitemap and robots.txt file.

1 In Google Webmaster Tools click the link for your site.

2 Click Site configuration.

3 Click a site configuration feature to find out more about it.

SEE ALSO: If no sitemap has been detected, install the Google XML Sitemaps plugin, as explained in Chapter 15. Open WordPress's Tools menu, click XML-Sitemap, and click the link to build the sitemap.

HOT TIP: Install a robots.txt plugin to generate a more detailed and useful robots.txt file than WordPress generates.

WHAT DOES THIS MEAN?

Sitemap: a list of Web pages that facilitates the process of indexing a site properly.

robots.txt: a file that tells search engines which files not to index.

View data in 'Your site on the Web'

Google Webmaster Tools features a 'Your site on the web' section that provides details on how your site appears to search engines and humans, plus how users reach your site.

1 In Google Webmaster Tools, click the link for your site.

2 Click Your site on the web on the menu.

3 Click a web metric to find out more about it.

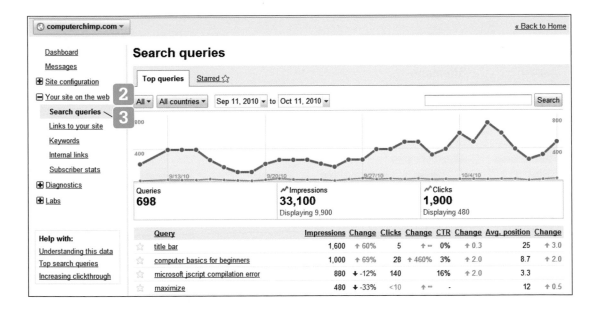

SEE ALSO: Your site on the web data is very useful for search engine optimisation (SEO). See Chapter 15 for more on this topic.

WHAT DOES THIS MEAN?

Web metric: a measurement of activity on a website.

Examine diagnostics for your site

If your site has errors that are preventing it from being indexed by search engines, you want to know about them and Google Webmaster Tools can help.

1 In Google Webmaster Tools, click the link for your site.

2 Click Diagnostics on the menu.

3 Click a diagnostic to find out more about it.

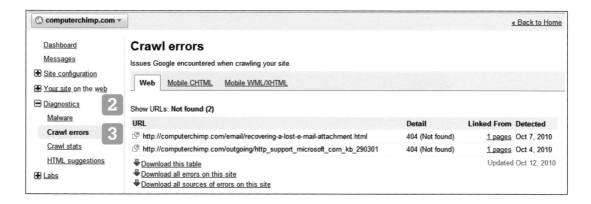

? DID YOU KNOW?
Diagnostics also checks for any malware on your site.

WHAT DOES THIS MEAN?
Malware: destructive computer code, including viruses.

Create a Google Analytics account

Google Analytics provides much more data about traffic on your site than you can obtain via Google Webmaster Tools. To get started, you must create an account.

1 Go to www.google.com/intl/en_uk/analytics and click Access Analytics.

2 Click Add new account.

3 Follow the onscreen instructions to set up your account.

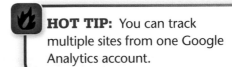

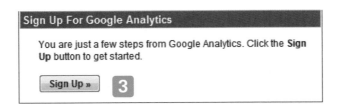

 SEE ALSO: Google Analytics will prompt you to enter your site's URL and lead you through the process of adding a tracking code to your site. See the next section for details.

HOT TIP: You can track multiple sites from one Google Analytics account.

ALERT: You will be asked to sign up for Google Analytics, but this is not like creating a new Google Account. You just need to add your name and site address and agree to the terms of service.

Add a Google Analytics tracking code to your site

To start collecting data, you must add a tracking code to your site.

1 In Google Webmaster Tools, click the link for your account.

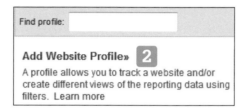

2 Click Add Website Profile.

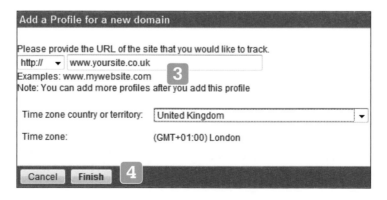

3 Type your site's address in the box.

4 Click Finish.

? DID YOU KNOW?

Google Analytics begins tracking traffic on your site immediately, but you probably will not see any data until the next day.

5 Copy the tracking code.

6 Paste the tracking code after the opening <head> tag in the Header (header.php) box or into the header box in your theme's control panel and save your changes.

❷ Paste this code on your site

Copy the following code, then paste it onto every page that you want to track immediately before the closing </head> tag. Learn more

```
<script type="text/javascript">

  var _gaq =
  _gaq.push(
  gaq.push(

  (function(
    var ga =
    ga.src =
    var s =
  }) ();

</script>
```

Undo	
Cut	5
Copy	
Paste	
Delete	
Select All	
🦎 Phoenix JS (5) CSS (1)	▶
Web Developer	▶
ColorZilla	▶
🗔 Inspect Element	

Header (header.php)   Select theme

```
<head>

<meta name="google-site-verification"
content="HOtPb4pIY8djhaV9qJdzfzqPhb6Y8Zsp9HItx_Cka3c" />

<script type="text/javascript">

  var _gaq = _gaq || [];
  _gaq.push(['_setAccount', 'UA-2176888-8']);
  _gaq.push(['_trackPageview']);              6

  (function() {
    var ga = document.createElement('script'); ga.type = 'text/javascript';
ga.async = true;
    ga.src = ('https:' == document.location.protocol ? 'https://ssl' :
'http://www') + '.google-analytics.com/ga.js';
    var s = document.getElementsByTagName('script')[0];
s.parentNode.insertBefore(ga, s);
  })();

</script>

</head>
```

Additional <head> scripts (code)

```
<script type="text/javascript">
  var _gaq = _gaq || [];       6
  _gaq.push(['_setAccount',
```

⚠ **ALERT:** The tracking code must appear between the opening and closing <head> tags near the top of the page. With some themes, you paste it in to the Header (header.php) box; in other themes, you add it via the theme's control panel.

Access Analytics for your site

After one or two days, sign in to your Google Analytics account and check the data that has been collected for your site.

1 Go to www.google.com/intl/en_uk/analytics and click Access Analytics.

2 Click your account.

Accounts							+ Add new account
Name↑	Visits	Avg. Time on Site	Bounce Rate	Completed Goals	Visits ▾	% Change	Actions
joekraynak.com **2**	3,246	00:01:04	81.73%	0	⬇ -0.82%		Edit

3 Click View report.

4 Explore the data and charts that appear.

Website Profiles							
Name↑		Reports	Status	Visits	Avg. Time on Site	Bounce Rate	Completed Goals
http://joekraynak.com UA-2176888-1 **3**							
☆ joekraynak.com		View report	✓	2,657	00:00:53	87.62%	0

HOT TIP: To return to the Overview: All Accounts page, click the Google Analytics logo in the upper left corner of any Analytics page you are on.

? DID YOU KNOW?

If you are tracking more than one site in an account, you can select a different site from the View Reports menu (near the top left of the screen) to view its reports.

HOT TIP: To find out more about a specific report, click the About this Report link in the Help Resources menu near the bottom of the left navigation bar.

17 Generate income from your site

Introduction

You have probably invested a great deal of hard work in building your first website, not to mention the money you are spending to host it. Perhaps you can recapture that investment and even earn a profit by using your site to generate income.

This chapter introduces you to several different ways to earn money with your site. It does not go into great detail on all the steps required to register and implement these money-making programs. In addition to having insufficient space to cover such tasks in detail, steps vary considerably depending on the products and services you choose to use.

Sell through affiliate programs

Many businesses on the Web offer affiliate programs. If someone clicks a link on your site to the business or a product or service it sells and places an order, you earn a small commission.

1 Sign up for an affiliate program and log on to your account.

2 Copy the code for adding a link to your site.

3 Paste the code on a page or post or in a text widget on your site.

Add pay-per-click advertisements

Google's AdSense enables website owners to place online advertisements on their sites and earn a commission when someone clicks an advertisement.

1 Sign up for an AdSense account and log in.

2 Create an ad according to your specifications.

3 Copy the code.

4 Paste the code on a page or post or in a text widget and click Save.

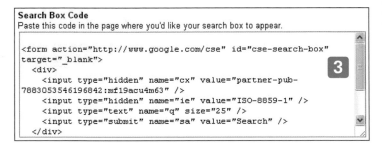

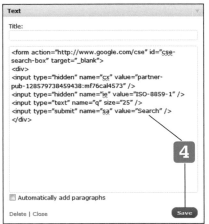

? DID YOU KNOW?

Unless you specify otherwise, the advertisement code determines which ads are most appropriate from your site's content.

► **SEE ALSO:** For more on widgets, see Chapter 8.

WHAT DOES THIS MEAN?

Pay-per-click (PPC) advertisements: online advertising that businesses pay for only if a user clicks the advertisement.

Add a PayPal shopping cart to your site

One of the easiest ways to sell products and services online is to enable PayPal to process your online payments.

1 Log in to your PayPal account and click the Merchant Services tab.

2 Click the Buy Now or Add to Cart Button link.

3 Create the button by selecting the options you want.

4 Copy the code.

5 Paste the code on a page or post or in a text widget and click Save.

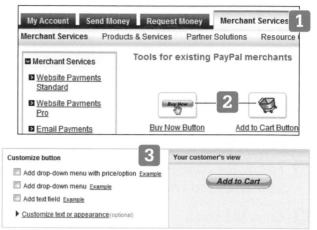

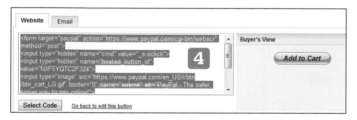

 ALERT: You must have a PayPal account to do this. Go to www.paypal.com/uk to open an account and log in.

HOT TIP: If you run an organisation that accepts donations, use an Add to Cart button to enable contributors to donate online.

? DID YOU KNOW?
Customers do not need a PayPal account to make a payment. With PayPal, you can accept credit card payments.

Coordinate your site with an eBay account

If you sell products via eBay, you can add the eBay To Go widget to a page, post or sidebar to showcase your eBay products.

1 Go to http://togo.ebay. com and click OK, LET'S GO!

2 Select your preferred version of the widget and click I WANT THIS ONE.

3 Follow the onscreen instructions to create the widget.

4 Copy the code.

5 Paste the code on a page or post or in a text widget and click Save.

? DID YOU KNOW?
If you have an eBay store, you can create a widget that links to products in your store.

Top 10 Website Problems Solved

Problem 1: I installed a WordPress plugin that messed up my site. What should I do?

If you are unsure which plugin is causing the problem, deactivate them one at a time starting with the plugin you most recently installed.

1 In WordPress, open the Plugins menu and click Plugins.

2 Click Deactivate.

3 If the problem persists, try deleting suspected plugins after deactivating them.

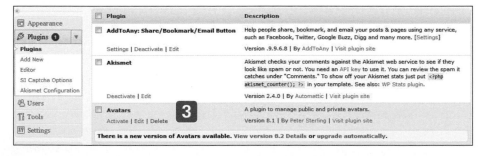

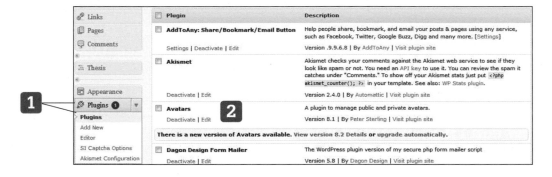

HOT TIP: After installing a plugin, wait a couple of days to see if everything is operating properly. This makes it easier to identify plugins that give you trouble.

Problem 2: I installed the W3 Total Cache plugin and am now getting an error message when I try to log in to WordPress. What should I do?

Installing the W3 Total Cache plugin may result in memory errors on your server that prevent you from logging in. Edit the php.ini file on your server, following the steps given below, to increase available memory.

1 Open your hosting provider's file manager and click the php.ini file.

2 Click the Edit button.

3 Change the memory_limit setting to 64M or 128M and save the file.

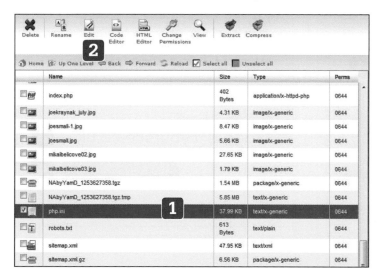

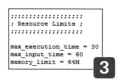

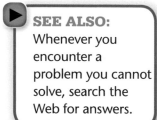

SEE ALSO: Whenever you encounter a problem you cannot solve, search the Web for answers.

ALERT: The php.ini file should be in the public_html folder.

HOT TIP: Use your browser's search feature to find 'memory_setting' in the php.ini file.

Problem 3: I forgot my username/password for logging in to WordPress. How can I find out what it is?

WordPress can send you your password via e-mail.

1 Access the WordPress Log in page.

2 Click Lost your password?

3 Type your username or e-mail address.

4 Click Get New Password.

 HOT TIP: If you forgot where to go to log in, access your hosting provider's account and check SimpleScripts or Fantastico to find out where you installed WordPress.

Problem 4: How do I move my site to a new domain without losing traction with search engines such as Google?

Create a 301 (permanent) redirect to let search engines know of your site's new location.

1 On the control panel, click Redirects.

2 Make sure Permanent (301) is selected.

3 Choose the domain you want to redirect.

4 To redirect a specific folder, type the path to the folder, including the folder's name.

5 Type the destination for the redirect, starting with 'http://'.

6 Click your www redirection preference, if available.

7 Click Wild Card Redirect to redirect all files in a directory to the same filenames in the redirects to folder.

8 Click Add.

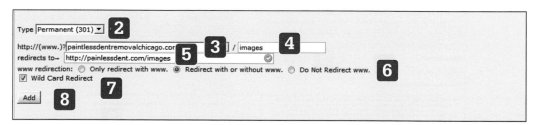

> **! ALERT:** The steps given here assume that you are logged in to your hosting account. See Chapter 2 for details.

> **? DID YOU KNOW?**
> A permanent (301) redirect updates the bookmarks in a visitor's browser and updates search engines. A temporary (302) redirect does not. Instead, it sends the browser to a different address, but browsers and search engines continue to try the original address in the future.

Problem 5: What could be causing my site to take so long to load in a Web browser?

You need to do some troubleshooting of your own to identify possible causes. The steps given below assume that you are using the Mozilla Firefox Web browser Firebug and the Google Page Speed plugin. See Chapters 11 and 14 for details.

1 Open the page you want to test in Firefox.

2 Click the Firebug icon.

3 Click Page Speed.

4 Click Analyze Performance.

5 Click a plus sign next to an issue to view details.

HOT TIP: Press F12 to run Firebug.

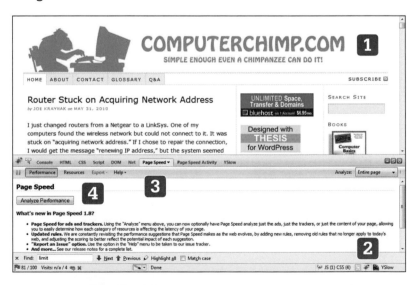

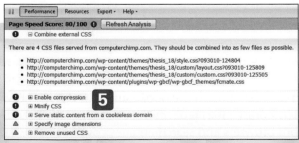

Problem 6: How do I add more space between an image and the text that wraps around it?

If text is too close to an image, edit the img selector's style rule to add a wider margin around the right side and bottom of the image.

1 In WordPress, open the Appearance menu and click Editor.

2 Open the theme's Stylesheet (style.css) file.

3 Add or edit the margin-right and margin-bottom properties to add space to the right side and bottom of the image and save your changes.

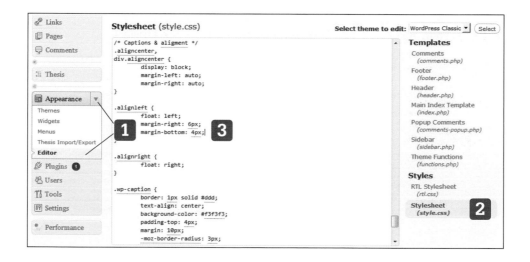

 ALERT: A theme's Stylesheet (style.css) file may have several img selectors for different alignment options, such as left (with text wrapping on the right) and right (with text wrapping on the left). Make sure that you edit the correct style rule.

Problem 7: I pasted the YouTube embed code on my page and, when I open the page, all I see is the code. How do I get the video to show?

You probably forgot to change to HTML view when pasting the embed code into the page or post.

1 In Visual mode, cut the embed code.

2 Click the HTML tab.

3 Paste the HTML tag back into the page or post and click Update.

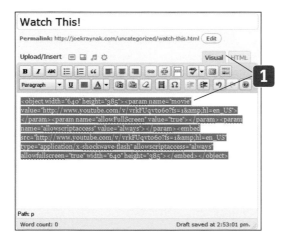

Problem 8: My sidebar appears below the content on my page. How do I move it up so that it appears alongside the content area?

Your columns are probably too wide for the space allotted in the theme. Use Firebug to troubleshoot the problem.

1 Open the page on which the problem occurs.

2 Click the Firebug icon.

3 Click the Inspect Element icon.

4 Click the container for the sidebar.

5 Click the width setting and type a smaller value to determine the value that works best.

6 Open your Stylesheet (style.css) file and enter the change.

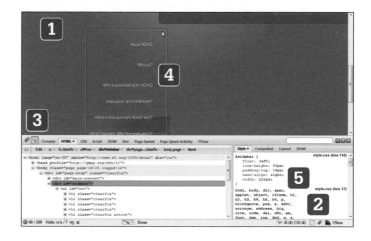

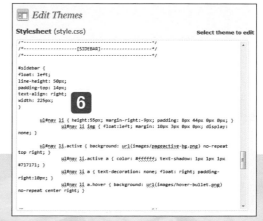

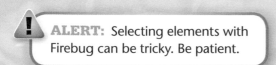

ALERT: Selecting elements with Firebug can be tricky. Be patient.

ALERT: Editing the sidebar's width in Firebug does not fix the problem; it only helps you to diagnose it. You must edit the value in your theme's Stylesheet (style.css) file.

Problem 9: How do I register my site with search directories?

Some search directories rely on the Open Directory Project for links to sites, so be sure you register your site at www.dmoz.org.

1 Go to www.dmoz.org/add.html.

2 Follow the step-by-step directions to suggest your site.

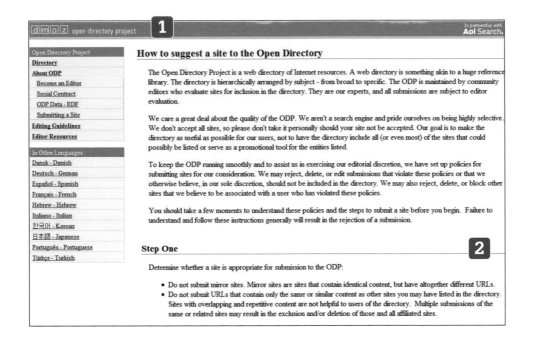

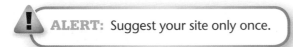

ALERT: Suggest your site only once.

ALERT: Search for your site on dmoz.org before suggesting it, so you do not create extra work for the indexers if it is already there.

Problem 10: How do I add an image to a sidebar in WordPress?

The easiest way to add an image to a sidebar in WordPress is to add the image tag to a text widget. Here's how.

1 Open the Appearance menu and click Widgets.

2 Expand the destination sidebar box.

3 Drag a text widget to the sidebar and drop it in place.

4 Type or paste an HTML image tag in the widget box.

5 Click Save.

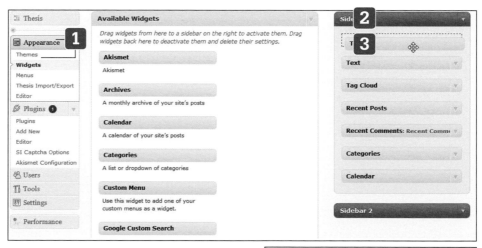

▶ **SEE ALSO:** You may need to adjust the style settings for the image in the widget to make it look right. See Chapter 11 for details on editing CSS style rules.

Use your computer with confidence

Office 2010
9780273736127

Excel 2010
9780273736134

Word 2010
9780273736141

Powerpoint 2010
9780273736158

Windows 7
9780273729136

Excel 2007
9780273723547

Office 2007
9780273723554

Laptop Basics Windows 7 Edition
9780273736806

Computer Basics Windows 7 edition
9780273736844

Windows Vista
9780273723493

Laptop Basics
9780273723486

Mac Basics
9780273729297

Computer Basics
9780273723479

Photoshop CS5
9780273736820

Photoshop Elements 8
9780273734390

Web Design
9780273723530

Netbook Basics
9780273734925

Windows 7 for the Over 50s
9780273729181

Laptop Basics for the Over 50s
9780273729129

Computer Basics for the Over 50s
9780273729174

in Simple steps

Practical. Simple. Fast.

PEARSON